THE COUNTRYSIDE COMPANION

Malcolm Tait
and
Olive Tayler

A THINK BOOK FOR

ROBSON BOOKS

The landscape is like a historic library of 50,000 books. Many were written in remote antiquity in languages, which have only lately been deciphered; some of the languages are still unknown.

Oliver Rackham

THINK

A Think Book
for Robson Books

First published in Great Britain in 2005 by
Robson Books
The Chrysalis Building, Bramley Road, London W10 6SP

An imprint of **Chrysalis** Books Group plc

Edited by Malcolm Tait and Olive Tayler
Companion team: Tilly Boulter, James Collins, Rhiannon Guy, Emma Jones,
Lou Millward, Matt Packer, Sonja Patel, Jo Swinnerton.

Think Publishing
The Pall Mall Deposit
124-128 Barlby Road, London W10 6BL
www.thinkpublishing.co.uk

ISBN 1-86105-918-3

Printed in Italy

Never make the mistake of thinking that the countryside is dull because there isn't a shop or a cinema at the corner of every winding lane.

Malcolm Saville

TRUE COUNTRY COMPANIONS

People without whom this book could not have
been written – not by a country mile:

My lifelong companion Claire Ashton Tait;
Zac Goldsmith, Peter Tait and James Tayler.

INTRODUCTION

The first thing to point out about this book is that it contains
several of the writings of members of my family. The memories of
various Taits, Taylers and Davises – some still with us, some no
longer – are recorded here as part of an overall view of the
countryside past and present, and for this I make no apology.
The countryside is almost entirely shaped by families, each
handing down from generation to generation their skills,
anecdotes, garments, implements, and general tricks of the trade
that have helped them survive off the land without depleting it.

To the country-dwellers of the past, the natural world around
them was a double-edged tool. Use it wisely, and it would keep
you and yours fed, watered and comfortable for generations. Use
it rashly, and it would cut you into little pieces. The natural
world is far better at dealing with radical change than we often
think, but while it's adjusting, it can't half make life difficult for
those who are trying to gain a living from it. Shoot all the rooks,
and there won't be any pie next year. Over-till the land, and it
won't support a single stalk of corn. Kill the golden goose, and
you'll soon be starving. Living in the country is about making
short-term decisions based on long-term thinking, and the Old
Folk knew that.

Some of these families still remain. And where they don't, as
often as not it's conservationists who have stepped in to look
after the land and the plants and creatures upon it. Yet the
countryside doesn't belong to any of them in particular, it
belongs to all of us, and we all belong to it. There is not one of
us without ancestors who lived off the land somewhere in the
world, and we must never forget that.

Not that this book is just a morality lesson. It's got plenty
of good gags in it too. But to my family, who played their part
in shaping the countryside, and in shaping me, I dedicate
The Countryside Companion.

Malcolm Tait, Editor

DARKLY SPEAKING

There are many who believe that the true accent, diction and language of the Black Country are among England's oldest. Here are some of the region's sayings:

I could a drapped cork-legged!
I was so surprised!

A bibble in a can.
A man who never stops talking.

This 'ay gettin the babbie a new bonnet.
This isn't getting the job done.

Ee cor stop a pig in an alley.
He is bow-legged.

Making a noise like a gleed under a door.
Singing badly.

It's a bit black over Bill's Mother's.
The weather looks bad in the distance.

Yo' soppy ha'p'orth.
You silly idiot.

We 'ad a bostin time.
We had a great time.

QUOTE UNQUOTE

A wealthy landowner cannot cultivate and improve his farm without spreading comfort and well-being around him. Rich and abundant crops, a numerous population and a prosperous countryside are the rewards for his efforts.
Antoine Lavoisier, French chemist

FUNNY FARM

A city type, on holiday in the country, meets up with a farmer and, betraying a lack of respect for rural folk, talks to him slowly and patronisingly. The farmer knows what's going on, but chats away nonetheless. Eventually, a swarm of flies starts buzzing around the tourist's head. 'Damn flies', he says, swatting at them. 'Do you know what type they are?'

'Aye, we call them circle flies around here.'

'Circle flies? Why's that?'

''Cause they're normally seen circling the rear end of a horse.'

'I see', says the tourist. Then, after a pause, the penny clicks. 'Hey, are you calling me the rear end of a horse.'

'Oh goodness me, no', says the farmer. 'I've far too much respect for you city folk than that.'

'Hmm, that's good', says the tourist, and carries on swatting. After a pause, the farmer leans forward and adds, 'Can't fool them flies, though.'

10 *Total length, in thousands of kilometres, of hedge planted in England and Wales between 1990 and 1998*

Climate change is happening, and year upon year it's becoming more dramatic. How it will affect our landscape and environments is difficult to predict, because the natural responses to the change will depend upon the exact pace of the warming of our climate. But results so far suggest that species are already on the move and altering their usual patterns. These changes will affect local ecosystems, which in turn affect landscapes and environments. Beech woods, for example, may struggle to respond to the different seasonal timings of what is going on around them, and steadily start to disappear. Similarly, the agricultural pockets of East Anglia might become too dry to farm effectively, shifting the farming centre of the UK further west and north.

So what precisely is happening so far? Research issued by the UK Phenology Network in 2005 has discovered the following:

- The long-winged conehead cricket, once restricted to the south coast, has moved 60 miles north.
- The red admiral butterfly, a migrating species, is now spending increasingly more winters in the UK.
- Frogs have started spawning before Christmas in the milder south west, as early even as October.
- In 2005, no fewer than 4,000 reports of bumblebee activity in January were reported.
- Daffodils have been flowering as early as Christmas Day.
- Oak trees have come into leaf three weeks earlier than they did in the 1950s.
- Grass now grows all year round, and a few reports have come in, even from Scotland, of grass that needed mowing in winter.

...AND JILL CAME CRUMBLING AFTERS

It's official! The nation's top dessert, according to a website poll by *Country Life*, is that rural favourite apple and blackcurrant crumble. Perhaps it's the appeal of being able to use real countryside produce that helped the tasty dish to the top of the pile, particularly as rhubarb crumble came second. Sticky toffee pudding and bread and butter pudding came in together in the bronze medal afters slot, closely followed by summer pudding and that suspicious incomer creme brulée.

Bottom of the list? Bakewell tart, ice cream and that urban dinner party favourite tiramisu. Ice cream down at the bottom? Perhaps the survey says more about the surfers of *Country Life* than puddings.

Talking of winter in April, which is now the rule, I am confirmed by Gray in my conviction that the times are changed. In 1755 the lime, he says, was in leaf at Cambridge on the 16th April; in 1763 on the 9th. There was not a sign of green upon mine this year until the first week in May. And so with most things. I have taken the trouble to study his lists. In January, February, March we are neck and neck; in some things fairly in advance. In April we drop behind, and never catch him up again. He had his fruit three weeks earlier than we ever do now. What is the meaning of that? I feel sure – and all the elderly weather-wise about here, shepherds, gamekeepers, carriers and the like, agree with me – that our winters have become our springs, and our springs our winters. A Christmas Number of the 'seventies, as I remember them, is not in touch with life as we know it now. The Squire's daughter, with her basket of buns and oranges for the deserving poor, would never need that snug red cloak, that muff of swansdown, those fur-edged boots. She would want them now for Easter Sunday. What has happened? I speak as a fool, but suggest the eruption of Mount Pelee in Martinique, throw it out like a bone for seismologists to mumble. Suppose that the levels of the sea-floor had been materially altered, might that not affect the Atlantic currents? If it did, might not that vary the dispersal of icebergs? I have understood that our cold weather depends upon the icebergs. That being so, the earlier those monsters come out the better.

Maurice Hewlett,
Wiltshire Essays, **1921**

DON'T HAVE A COW, MAN

Bovine superstitions that you might want to be aware of:

- Cattle should be told of deaths in their owners' household, otherwise they might sicken and die themselves.
- It is unlucky to offer to buy cattle that are not for sale. It's also unlucky to strike a cow with your bare hands: you should herd them with a stick.
- If cattle stand on low ground, then rain is coming. High ground means that the weather will be fair.
- To protect your cattle from disease, attach a horseshoe over the door of their stall, or drip wax from an Easter candle on their horns and the entrance to the stall.
- It is unlucky to meet a herd of cattle on the road.
- If a cow breaks into your garden, there will be a death in the family.
- Kill crane flies with your plough, and dry will be your cow.

A HELPING HAND

Champions of the countryside in their own words:

THE WILDFOWL & WETLANDS TRUST (WWT) is the largest international wetland conservation charity in the UK.

WWT's mission is to conserve wetlands and their biodiversity. These are vitally important for the quality and maintenance of all life.

Founded in 1946 by the artist and naturalist Sir Peter Scott (1909 – 1989), WWT has nine visitor centres, covering around 2000 hectares in Northern Ireland, Scotland, Wales and England, where people can get closer to wetland birds and enjoy spectacular wetland landscapes in a welcoming and friendly environment.

www.wwt.org.uk

COUNTRY CONUNDRUMS

By rearranging the letters, which TV programme
should this person present?
TONY LUCIFER
Answer on page 153.

MEMORIES AND CONVERSATION

Reminiscences of southern counties country life, as recorded by George Sturt in the late nineteenth century from conversations with his gardener, whom he called Bettesworth:

'Always a good 'n for work, was Edmund. He used always to get up Sundays jest same as week-days; it didn't make no difference – about four or five o'clock he was up, feedin' and workin'. But there, that was his way: he was reg'lar. He had his time for gettin' up an' for gwine to bed too, an' he never altered. When the time come at night, he was up and off... But he's gone now, poor old feller. They seems to allow he've put some ha'pence together, too. They don't know, but they thinks so. There's they six houses, ye see. Well, an' so he ought, if you come to that. He never was a wasteful, 'xtrav-agant kind o' feller. In his food, now, 'twas always wonderful plain; good, ye know, but noth-in' flash about it; not this way one day an' that 'nother, but same as gwine to bed – re'lar... Why, he never got married not afore he was – what now? – fifty, I reckon. An' then he married two sisters. One of 'em first; an' when she died then he took t'other. The vicar, he was down on 'n for that; but Edmund says, "Well, if I didn't marry her, somebody else would"'.

The Bettesworth Book,
written 1896

*Unlike his white cousin, the brown rabbit
always had time for a pretty girl.*

NOTHING NEW UNDER THE SUN

*Techy types may think they invented a new language, but no. Here are
the real meanings behind the terminology that the computer industry
has adopted:*

Download	Get the wood off the cart
Log on	Make a wood stove hotter
Log off	Cool it down again
Mega hertz	When you're not too careful about logging on and off
Floppy disc	From carrying too much wood
Hard drive	Getting back to the farm in winter
Lap top	Where the farm cat sleeps
Software	A good hat for keeping out the cold
Mouse	Eats all the grain
Mouse pad	Catches the mice that eat all the grain
Main frame	Supports the barn roof
Modem	What was done to the fields

*It's only the urban middle-class who worry about the preservation
of the countryside, because they don't have to live in it.*
Sir Humphrey Appleby, *Yes Minister.*

KINGDOM FOR A HORSE

*Alderley Edge in Cheshire is well known for its deep caves, mined
since the bronze age and now a caver's delight. But if you want to
explore them, beware. One ancient legend reveals who you might
stumble across...*

Once, a farmer from Mobberley was on his way to Macclesfield Market to sell a white mare. The horse was the finest of his stock, and he was sure that he could get a good price at the market.

As he passed by the steep sandstone cliffs that make up Alderley Edge, he was stopped by an old man of noble stature with a white beard, and clothes that seemed to belong to an earlier period of history. The old man asked if the farmer would sell his horse to him for a fair price. The farmer refused, hoping that he could get a better price for such a fine animal at the market.

Once at the bustling market it seemed as though he had been bewitched. Although his animal was admired and commented on, not a single offer was made, although lesser animals were sold quickly for good prices.

Dejected the farmer set off back to Mobberley. As he passed Alderley Edge the same old man appeared and asked if he could buy the horse. The farmer agreed and the wizard motioned him to follow, leading the farmer through trees to the foot of the sandstone cliffs that make up the edge. The

wizard touched the rock with his staff, and the rock parted with a thunderous sound to reveal a huge cavern. The old man led the farmer inside the earth reassuring him not to be afraid.

The farmer could not believe his eyes, for inside the cavern hundreds of armour-clad warriors lay in a deathly sleep. Every warrior bar one had a white horse standing next to him. The old man (who seemed now to be a wizard of great power) explained that these men were King Arthur and his knights who were ready and waiting for the day when their countrymen would need them, then they would arise and fight to save the country. The wizard led on to a pile of gold and jewels, and told the farmer to take his fill as payment for his mare.

The farmer grabbed a handful of golden coins and jewels, stuffed them into his pockets and walked out through the opening into the bright sunlight. The farmer, overwhelmed by his strange experience, set off running as the rock closed with a dull thud behind him. Although he tried, neither he nor anyone else could ever find the door again.

LAST CHANCE TO SEE

One of the most powerful working horses in Britain is also one of the rarest. The Suffolk punch, which numbered in its thousands in East Anglia in the early part of the twentieth century, was down to just 70 breeding females by the end of it. Whether working the land or drawing carts, the Suffolk was a tireless, good-natured creature. But as agricultural mechanisation crept into the flat lands of the east, where landowners were often rich enough to be able to afford it, so the heavy horse's duties dwindled. Every modern representative of this strong breed was descended from a single individual – Crisp's Horse of Ufford, foaled in 1768 – and can be distinguished by its chesnut coat (interestingly, always spelt, when describing this breed, without the 't').

NUL POINTS

British fungi that sound like entrants in the *Eurovision Song Contest*:
Sandy stiltball
Lemon disco
Smoky bracket
Ruby bolete
Prunes and custard
Giant puffball
Willow bracket
The gypsy
Apricot club
Cinnamon jellybaby

LUCKY CLUCK

Some countryside tales are apocryphal, others are dubious, but some, and perhaps the most bizarre of all, are completely true. Witness the tale of the chicken that was found in Cheshire in 2003 by the side of the road, near to death. The passer-by took the chicken home, and brought her back to life. One lucky chicken! About a week later the owner started wondering whether his new feathered friend's good luck might be contagious. He offered the bird his calculator, and it tapped out a series of numbers. Entering them onto his lottery ticket, five of them came up, and the household benefited to the tune of no less than £1,300. One lucky owner!

Lucky the chicken – as she unsurprisingly became named – went on to live happily at her new home in a coop for several months... until her fortunes finally changed. One night when the coop was unlocked, a fox slipped in, and Lucky and her luck were no more.

COUNTRY CONTEMPLATIONS

The Devil never keeps his bargains. Many years ago he struck one with a Devonshire brewer named Frankan, who, it is said, was alarmed at the effect the new cult of cider-drinking was having on his trade. So he sold his soul to the Devil in return for frosts on May 19th, 20th and 21st sufficiently hard to ruin the apple-blossom. In recent years the Devil has been observing his side of the contract only half-heartedly; in 1978 and again in 1980 he ignored it entirely.

Everywhere the trees were loaded, with branches splitting under the weight of fruit. The gales of early September littered the ground beneath the trees with fallen fruit, yet the crop left on the trees still seemed undiminished.

A traveller can estimate his distance from London by observing the hand-painted advertisements for apples at roadside farmsteads and gardens. Near the capital the posters advertise 'WINDFALL APPLES' at so much per pound. Farther out, the captions change to 'WINDFALLS' or, more often, 'FALLERS'. But when he sees a sign saying simply 'MORGAN SWEETS', he knows he is in the West Country. Who, apart from a West Countryman, would know that Morgan Sweet is an apple?

Ralph Whitlock, *The Countryside: Random Gleanings*

HARVEST CROON

Agriculturalists who made it into song:

Melon Farmer .... Ash
Farmer Ferdinand Hudson .... Bee Gees
Me and the Farmer .... Housemartins
Farmer John .... Neil Young
Frances Farmer Will Have her Revenge on Seattle .... Nirvana
Taxes on the Farmer Feeds Us All .... Ry Cooder
Now I'm a Farmer .... The Who

HOW TO LAY YOUR ROOF WITH COTSWOLD STONE SLATES

Fix wooden battens, or laths, along the roof from which to hang the slates. Decrease the distance between each batten by half an inch from the bottom upwards, as each row of slates is slightly shorter than the one below it. Remember that the slant of a stone roof is only about 50 degrees, compared with the 65 degrees required for thatch.

Having drilled holes into the slates, drive an oak peg into them and then hang them over the battens. Then cap the finished roof with an angled section of dressed stone. Stand back and admire for the next 300 years.

BIT GUSTY OUT

The Beaufort scale was devised by Admiral Sir Francis Beaufort in 1805 to estimate wind strengths. It's useful to know for when you want to describe your walk in the country properly. The scale for use on land is as follows:

Force	Mph	Description	
0	0-1	Calm	*Smoke rises vertically.*
1	1-3	Light air	*Direction of wind shown by smoke drift, but not by wind vanes.*
2	4-7	Light Breeze	*Wind felt on face; leaves rustle; ordinary vanes moved by wind.*
3	8-12	Gentle Breeze	*Leaves and small twigs in constant motion; wind extends light flag.*
4	13-18	Moderate Breeze	*Raises dust and loose paper; small branches are moved.*
5	19-24	Fresh Breeze	*Small trees in leaf begin to sway.*
6	25-31	Strong Breeze	*Large branches in motion; whistling heard in telegraph wires.*
7	32-38	Near Gale	*Trees in motion; inconvenience felt when walking against the wind.*
8	39-46	Gale	*Twigs break off trees; walking becomes difficult.*
9	47-54	Severe Gale	*Slight structural damage occurs (chimney-pots and slates removed).*
10	55-63	Storm	*Seldom experienced inland; trees uprooted; structural damage.*
11	64-72	Violent Storm	*Very rarely experienced; accompanied by wide-spread damage.*
12	73-83	Hurricane	*Good luck.*

ALAN THE SHEARER

How long does it take to shear a sheep? It depends on whether the *Guinness Book of Records* is watching. They were there for Alan MacDonald and Keith Wilson's attempt on the record in New Zealand in 1988, and they saw the two men machine-shear an extraordinary total of 2,220 of the creatures in a single 24-hour period – that's just a little under 100 sheep per hour (92.5 to be precise). The shearathon raised over NZ$10,000 for charity.

THE OTHER ARCHER

Not all rural *Archers* are fictional. Fred of that name (1915-1999) was a farmer from the Vale of Evesham, who in 1967 was persuaded by his family to send his reminiscences and country tales to a publisher, so much did they enjoy them. He did so, and *The Distant Scene* was published to great success, launching for this man of the soil a new career in writing. He published nearly a book a year over the next three decades, with titles like *Hawthorn Farm*, *Country Sayings*, *A Country Twelvemonth* and *The Village of My Childhood*. Filling his books with memories of the folk he grew up, played and worked with, Archer's writing was respectful, twinkling and humorous, drawing admiration from the likes of Auberon Waugh and Laurie Lee. 'I felt it would be such a pity if, when these characters died, their sayings, customs, ways of life, how they dressed, should vanish with them', he once said. Thanks to Fred, they never will.

WHAT'S IN A NAME: B

Badger	Licensed pauper, or corn dealer
Barleyman	Manorial court official (byelawman)
Baxter	Baker
Bedman	Sexton
Bender	Leather cutter
Bodger	Maker of chair legs
Boniface	Innkeeper
Bowdler	Worker with iron ore
Bowker	Yarn bleacher. Alternatively, a butcher

COUNTRY CONTEMPLATIONS

The river winds its narrow tortuous course between low level meadows or rushy banks. Stunted water-willows overhang cool deep pools – a paradise for bathers. Here a trio of meditative anglers moor their punt athwart the stream; there a camper pitches his white-coned tent. Black and dun cattle wading in the shallow; an old bridge or riverside inn; long weirs and narrow locks – are the chief incidents in a day's progress. If there is less variety in the scenery than lower down the river there are also fewer interruptions to its quiet beauty. Lechlade seen across low meadows, with the spire of St Lawrence's; the Wytham woods; a few reaches of peculiar beauty at Bablockhythe or Northmoor, may remain most clearly in the memory, but they stand in no sharp contrast to the scenery before and after them.

JH and JA Salter, *Salter's Guide to the Thames*, 1930s.
From the chapter 'The Source to Oxford'

FLOCK FOR LUCK

Sheep play quite a prominent role in folklore, some beliefs more gruesome than others:

- To meet a flock of sheep on a journey is an omen of good luck.
- Sheep that lie peacefully in the field herald fine weather, but rain is foretold if they are restless and noisy.
- If sheep gnash their teeth during round-up in the autumn, the winter will be hard. If sheep gnash their teeth somewhere else, it presages very bad weather.
- If you carry a knuckle-bone from a piece of mutton in your pocket it becomes a charm against rheumatism.
- Carry a T-shaped bone from a sheep's head to protect yourself from bad luck and evil.
- Wrap yourself in the skin of a freshly killed sheep to cure adder bites.
- If your child has whooping-cough, they can be cured by letting a sheep breathe on them.
- Got consumption? Walk around a flock of sheep several times a day.
- If you want to break a curse, stick a sheep's heart full of pins and roast it at midnight in a room where all doors, windows and openings have been closed.

QUOTE UNQUOTE

*Farming looks mighty easy when your plough is a pencil
and you're a thousand miles from the cornfield.*
Dwight D Eisenhower, US President

ON THE WING, IN THE WINGS

It doesn't take too long, if you're patient and have a decent ear, to work out the springtime melodies of each of the birds of the countryside. The piercing notes of the great tit, the melancholic warbling of the robin, the machine-gun rattle of the wren... but wait, what's that? A throaty little gargle that sounds a bit like, well, several birds? This is the tricky world of the subsong – effectively a watered down, erratic, quieter version of the bird's main theme that acts as a prelude to the full-on rendition. It sounds as if the bird is going over its lines while waiting in the wings.

One of the best descriptions was by DP Snow in his *Study of Blackbirds*: 'Males utter a subdued version of the song, hurried and confused and strongly giving the impression that the bird is prevented from singing normally by being strangled.'

LAST CHANCE TO SEE

Now down to just a couple of hundred individuals, Exmoor ponies have been on the moors since ancient times, surviving so long thanks to their great hardiness, lengthy winter coat and strong spirit. It's unlikely that the horse has changed much since the Stone Age, bones having been found in the Mendips identical to those of today's animals, just 12,000 years older! The independent little horse, however, which stands at around 12 hands high, does have a future. It is now being bred in many places in Britain, and used by organisations like The Wildlife Trusts, the National Trust and English Nature to graze reserves, thanks to its willingness to tackle coarse plants. Perhaps surprisingly, given its independent nature, it can be brought well to harness and is a good family horse.

THE NAMING OF SHERWOOD

Sherwood Forest, home to Robin Hood, Little John et al, is first recorded in 958AD as 'Sciryuda', meaning 'the woodland belonging to the shire'. (It didn't stay that way long, however, becoming one of several hunting forests claimed for the crown by William the Conqueror in the late eleventh century.)

CAT CALLS

Big cats in the countryside: fact or myth? According to the British Big Cat Society (BBCS), whose slogan is 'Prove and Protect', they're most definitely a fact, with over 2,000 reported sightings between January 2003 and March 2004. But then, such an organisation, and the people who contact them, would believe, wouldn't they? Well, how about the Humberside police, then, who in September 2003 became the first force to publicly announce that they, too, believed that big cats were roaming our land. Following several reports of sightings around the Yorkshire Wolds, and the killing of several sheep as they slept, the force came to the conclusion that there were probably two cats, possibly panthers, patrolling territories that matched in size those of their native lands. In fact, one owner of big cats in the area even admitted to the police that he was planning to release his animals so that he could hunt them.

The evidence appears to be mounting. Meanwhile, if you're wondering if there's anything prowling around up the road from you, here are the top ten areas in terms of sightings as recorded by the BBCS during their monitoring period: Scotland (231); Kent (141); Yorkshire (127); Wales (102); Devon (100); Cornwall (96); Lancashire (86); Ireland (82); Lincolnshire (80); and Somerset (69).

A HELPING HAND

Champions of the countryside in their own words:

BTCV is the UK's largest practical conservation charity. Founded in 1959, we help over 130,000 volunteers take hands-on action each year to improve the rural and urban environment.

We offer:

- Practical conservation opportunities
- Support and advice for local people and community groups
- UK and International Conservation Holidays
- Training and learning opportunities
- Practical land management for conservation
- Opportunities for young people to develop skills and careers
- Employment programmes to give people the skills for work
- Recycling and waste minimisation projects and consultancy
- Environmental consultancy and project management
- Mail order delivery, including trees, wildflowers, tools and handbooks

www.btcv.org

COUNTRY CONUNDRUMS

A farmer has a quarter of a haystack in one corner of a field, two-thirds of a haystack in another, a sixth of a haystack in the third corner, and two-fifths of a haystack in the last corner. He brings them all into the middle of the field.

How many haystacks does he have?

Answer on page 153.

KEEP YOUR BODY DRY

Lychgates are part of the countryside scene: a rural church barely seems right without one. Yet the origin of the name and the feature itself was more practical than ornamental. The Saxon word 'lych' meant 'corpse', for the gate was the initial resting place of the deceased.

During the middle ages, when most people were buried in simple shrouds rather than coffins, their bodies were carried as far as the lychgate where they remained until the priest was ready to start the funeral service under the protection of the covered archway. First built around the fifteenth century, most lychgates were wooden and supported by four or six oaken posts driven into the ground. In later years, stone was more frequently used.

NATURALLY SPEAKING

The *New Naturalist* series of books published by Collins has, since 1945, been producing on average nearly two titles a year, each contributing to a steadily building library of invaluable information on British and Irish wildlife. Most of the 95 books published by 2005 examine wildlife groups, as broad as the *Natural History of Pollination*, or as focused as *British Tits*. Some, however, deal with particular regions. They are:

COUNTRY CONTEMPLATIONS

As the weather worsened I yearned to tune into some ancestral rite, some spell to deter the insidious onset of winter. First the fog came down, at just the moment East Anglian farmers began taking in the sugar-beet, and turned the harvest of this noxious crop into high drama. The immense machines, as tall as houses, worked on into the darkness, with racks of headlights glowing palely through the mist. From my study window it looked like a scene from Close Encounters. The beet-stack next to the farmhouse swelled until it was more like a wartime fortification than a pile of vegetables. The next day the harvesters were joined by tractor-drawn ploughs and harrows and drills, until there were often three different machines following each other round the fields. Hares scattered towards the hedges and fugitive pheasants lined up on our wall. Within two weeks the winter wheat was already a mist of green over the bare soil.

Richard Mabey, *Nature Cure*

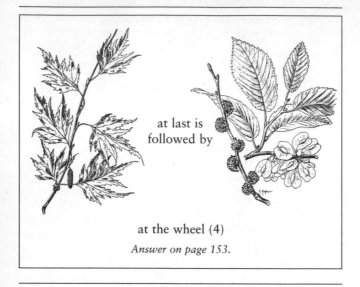

at last is
followed by

at the wheel (4)

Answer on page 153.

QUOTE UNQUOTE

Agriculture not only gives riches to a nation,
but the only riches she can call her own.
Samuel Johnson, man of letters

ANIMAL MADJECTIVE

Here's how to impress your fellow countryside wanderers. Mention that cervine herd, or that leporine fight, or a limacine trail, and gain admiration for the rest of your days. Here are the animals that go with those adjectives, and more:

Crab	*cancrine*
Deer	*cervine*
Dormouse	*myoxine*
Hare	*leporine*
Lizard	*lacertilian*
Seal	*phocine*
Shrew	*soricine*
Slug	*limacine*
Toad	*batrachian*
Vole	*microtine*

Sir Thomas More (1478–1535) explains the function of the countryside in *Utopia*:

Of these cities they that be nighest together be twenty-four miles asunder. Again there is none of them distant from the next above one day's journey afoot. There come yearly to Amaurote out of every city three old men wise and well experienced, there to entreat and debate, of the common matters of the land. For this city (because it standeth just in the midst of the island, and is therefore most meet for the ambassadors of all parts of the realm) is taken for the chief and head city. The precincts and bounds of the shires be so commodiously appointed out, and set forth for the cities, that never a one of them all hath of any side less than twenty miles of ground, and of some side also much more, as of that part where the cities be of farther distance asunder. None of the cities desire to enlarge the bounds and limits of their shires. For they count themselves rather the good husbands than the owners of their lands.

They have in the country in all parts of the shire houses or farms builded, well appointed and furnished with all sorts of instruments and tools belonging to husbandry. These houses be inhabited of the citizens, which come thither to dwell by course. No household or farm in the country hath fewer than forty persons, men and women, besides two bondmen, which be all under the rule and order of the good man, and the good wife of the house, being both very sage and discreet persons. And every thirty farms or families have one head ruler, which is called a philarch, being as it were a head bailiff. Out of every one of these families or farms cometh every year into the city twenty persons which have continued two years before in the country.

In their place so many fresh be sent thither out of the city, which of them that have been there a year already, and be therefore expert and cunning in husbandry, shall be instructed and taught. And they the next year shall teach other. This order is used for fear that either scarceness of victuals, or some other like incommodity should chance, through lack of knowledge, if they should be altogether new, and fresh, and unexpert in husbandry. This manner and fashion of yearly changing and renewing the occupiers of husbandry, though it be solemn and customably used, to the intent that no man shall be constrained against his will to continue long in that hard and sharp kind of life, yet many of them have such a pleasure and delight in husbandry, that they obtain a longer space of years. These husbandmen plough and till the ground, and breed up cattle, and make ready wood, which they carry to the city either by land, or by water, as they may most conveniently.

They bring up a great multitude of poultry, and that by a marvellous policy. For the hens do not sit upon the eggs: but by keeping them in a certain equal heat they bring life into them, and hatch them. The chickens, as soon as they be come out of the shell, follow men and women instead of the hens. They bring up very few horses: nor none, but very fierce ones: and for none other use or purpose, but only to exercise their youth in riding and feats of arms. For oxen be put to all the labour of ploughing and drawing. Which they grant to be not so good as horses at a sudden brunt, and (as we say) at a dead lift, but yet they hold opinion that they will abide and suffer much more labour and pain than horses will.

And they think that they be not in danger and subject unto so many diseases and that they be kept and maintained with much less cost and charge: and finally that they be good for meat, when they be past labour. They sow corn only for bread. For their drink is either wine made of grapes, or else of apples, or pears, or else it is clean water. And many times mead made of honey or liquorice sodden in water, for thereof they have great store. And though they know certainly (for they know it perfectly indeed) how much victuals the city with the whole country or shire round about it doth spend: yet they sow much more corn, and breed up much more cattle, than serveth for their own use, and the overplus they part among their borderers. Whatsoever necessary things be lacking in the country, all such stuff they fetch out of the city: where without any exchange they easily obtain it of the magistrates of the city. For every month many of them into the city on the holy day. When their harvest day draweth near and is at hand, then the philarchs, which be the head officers and bailiffs of husbandry, send word to the magistrates of the city what number of harvest men is needful to be sent to them out of the city. The which company of harvest men being there ready at the day appointed, almost in one fair day despatcheth all the harvest work.

GOOSEBERRY GOODNESS

The gooseberry, a favourite garden plant, is almost certainly a native plant to Britain, and from July onwards can be found in old woodlands in decent numbers. Cultivation of the fruit didn't start until the late sixteenth century, and within 300 years around 2,000 varieties had been developed – but the wild gooseberry is still one of the tastiest and tangiest fruits of the forest. To make your own gooseberry fool, stew a cup of them, topped and tailed, in two glasses of white wine and a dollop of honey until you have reduced the mixture to a sticky goo. Allow it to cool, then fold in a quarter cup of whipped cream. Sit back, eat at leisure, and give thanks for the natural flavours of the countryside.

FUNNY FARM

A man is driving along a country road one morning, when he loses control of his steering and drives straight into a ditch. Looking around, he sees a farmer leading an old carthorse home, so he calls out for help, and the farmer wanders over. He eyes up the situation, and attaches his horse, Boxer, to the car's bumper.

'Heave-ho, Jasper', he shouts, but Boxer doesn't move a muscle.

He shouts again. 'Heave-ho, Samson.' Again, Boxer just stands still.

Finally he shouts, 'Heave-ho, Boxer', and the old horse strains against the ropes and slowly pulls out the car.

'That was fantastic, thank you', gushes the man, 'but one question. Why did you call your horse by three different names?'

'Ah', says the farmer, 'poor old Boxer, he's blind, see, and if he thought he were the only one pulling, he wouldn't have bothered.'

BRITISH MOTHS OF CHARACTER

The nonconformist
The suspected
The confused
The uncertain
The delicate
The stranger
The basker
The gothic

RIGHT CHARLIE

Few people realise that in the run-up to the 2005 General Election, the Labour Party approached Prince Charles with a deal. The idea was that the Prince would in effect become the 'countryside tsar' during a third-term Labour government, helping to smooth relations over with rural voters disenchanted by the government's handling of foot and mouth, BSE and fox hunting. In return, the hands-on experience of working in a particular public sector would give the Prince good grounding in his preparation to become king. Charles himself was reported to have made it a condition of the job that the government would overturn its ban on fox hunting, rebranding it as a sport for the many, not the few. Another part of the package was that the long-running radio serial, *The Archers*, would finally make the transition to TV – Channel Five to be exact.

If anyone would like to know further details about the deal, the story was reported in *The Guardian* on 1 April 2005.

COUNTRY CONTEMPLATIONS

When silver snow decks Sylvio's clothes
And jewel hangs at shepherd's nose,
We can abide life's pelting storm
That makes our limbs quake, if our hearts be warm.

Whilst Virtue is our walking-staff
And Truth a lantern to our path,
We can abide life's pelting storm
That makes our limbs quake, if our hearts be warm.

Blow, boisterous wind, stern winter frown,
Innocence is a winter's gown;
So clad, we'll abide life's pelting storm
That makes our limbs quake, if our hearts be warm.

William Blake, *Song by an Old Shepherd,*
The Good Life

QUOTE UNQUOTE

The hot day is the first day of summer. The day when
you realise that there can be too much sunshine, the day when
the heat strikes up from bare soil and reflects back from walls
and buildings, the day, above all others, when you can
truthfully say, 'Thank goodness I am not in a town.'
Ralph Wightman, farmer and broadcaster

'OW TO LOOK AFTER YER FERRET

- Ferrets require a dark enclosed sleeping box with a 8.5 centimetre diameter entrance hole and ventilation at the top, and a toilet area that has a wood-shaving base. You need to clean it every day.
- If the cage is outside, ensure the sleeping area is raised well clear of the ground to eliminate damp.
- If you're using wire mesh for the cage, make it at least 16-gramme weld mesh: ferrets can break through ordinary chicken wire.
- Make sure the housing is strong and secure. Ferrets use their teeth and sharp claws to pull at loose edges. Don't leave any gaps as ferrets are born Houdinis: give them an inch and they'll run a mile.
- Bedding should be of clean hay or straw, old clothing or shredded paper. Change it regularly.
- Despite the rumours, ferrets derive no particular pleasure from living down your trousers.

Thanks to the amount of light given off by streetlamps, all-night garages and security lights, only the brightest of stars are visible in towns. Orion, the hunter, is one of the few constellations that can be seen in urban areas, but step out to the darker countryside and you can really see him in detail. According to mythology, Artemis, goddess of the hunt, had fallen in love with Orion, which didn't please her brother Apollo. One day, Apollo saw Orion swimming far out at sea, so challenged his sister to fire her arrow and hit the distant dot among the waves. She did so and having found that she'd killed her beloved, placed his body in the heavens together with his hunting dogs.

The constellation, best seen between December and April, is easily identified by Orion's belt, a line of three bright stars (Alnitak, Alnilam and Mintaka), the central one of which is about 10,000 times more luminous than the sun. The hunter's right shoulder, a reddish star, is Betelgeuse, while his left knee is Rigel. As you watch him cross the night sky from east to west, you can see that his two faithful hounds, Canis Major and Canis Minor, follow him.

He's been recognised for thousands of years, known by the Chaldeans of Mesopotamia as Tammuz, after the hebrew month in which his belt first becomes visible. In Syria he was known as Al Jabbar, the Giant, while the Egyptians saw him as Sahu, the soul of Osiris. The Sumerians, however, thought he was a sheep.

WORKING DOGS

Pointers

These are dogs best suited to open grouse moors, where the game is distributed far and wide. Circling the moors, they locate their prey through sight and sound, and then rather than dash in, stare – or point – directly at it. The hunter moves in and when he is close enough, the dog goes for the flush. Initially bred as a rabbit hunter, the pointer first took to the moors in the eighteenth century, where it often worked in pairs, the two 'points' helping the hunter pinpoint the quarry more accurately.

Its ancestry is unclear, probably arising from Spanish pointers of the sixteenth and seventeenth centuries. The problem with the early pointers, however, was that they were too slow, and by the late eighteenth century they were being bred with foxhounds for that extra turn of speed. This wasn't a complete success, as the dogs became too fond of chasing the game themselves, so by the nineteenth century the setter was introduced to the bloodline, making them easier to train.

Number of times the word 'fields' is mentioned in The Complete Works 29
of Shakespeare

A HELPING HAND

Champions of the countryside in their own words:

FARM is a campaign group bringing together farmers, consumers and environmentalists to fight for a sustainable future for farming in the UK.

We exist to stop the demise of the farming industry and to bring true sustainability to farming policy and practice, such that agriculture is able to deliver its full potential of economic, social and environmental benefits to society.

We believe that long-term sustainability will only come about if farming is:

- economically viable
- diverse, evolving and well-populated
- delivering sustainability in farming practice

whilst, all along, engaging with the general public

www.farm.org.uk

DOWN ON THE FILM

Movies that might disappoint fans of agriculture:
Silence of the Lambs, 1991
Poor Cow, 1967
They Shoot Horses, Don't They?, 1969
As Ye Sow, 1912
Hog Wild, 1980
Raging Bull, 1980
The Sign of the Ram, 1948

IF YOU'RE HAPPY, WAGYU TAIL

There are burgers, and there are burgers, but the Wagyu burger, served in some London restaurants, and made of the beef that comes from the Wagyu cattle bred in Kobe, Japan, is perhaps the king of them all. Sampling one may set you back at least 50 quid, and if you're wondering why, the delicately marbled meat that goes to make it is only part of the story. The Japanese look after their cattle in a way rarely seen in the British countryside. For a start, they massage their cows to give them a life free of stress. But life needs to be enjoyable as well as stress-free, so they give their cattle beer to drink as well. And to top off the perfect bovine existence, the herds are serenaded with sweet music at various times of the day. Now that's farming with the softest of touches.

GREAT LOOPHOLES OF OUR TIME

Sites of Special Scientific Interest (SSSIs) are not necessarily nature reserves, but areas of land use that are important for conservation reasons. They might be examples of rare habitat, or perhaps they're home to a vulnerable species. Whatever the reason for their designation, they were first created by the Nature Conservancy Council 'to form a national network of areas representing in total those parts of Great Britain in which the features of nature, and especially those of greatest value to wildlife conservation, are most highly concentrated or of highest quality'.

As land that is designated SSSI can belong to anyone, it has to undergo a proposal process before it receives the protection (up to a £20,000 fine for its destruction) that it requires. And here lay the loophole. During the proposal period – which lasted three months – the site still had no protection, and by the early 1980s, some landowners who were worried that an SSSI designation would compromise what they wanted to do with their land, simply disposed of whatever it was that made their site worthy of protection.

The whole process was in danger of collapsing. What's the good of protecting an area from development if you give the developers a three-month head start to legally dispose of the reason for its protection? The loophole was finally closed in a 1985 amendment to the Wildlife and Countryside Act 1981, giving proposed SSSIs protection during the proposal period, too.

PEAK PRACTICE

Each year, hardy souls raise hundreds of thousands of pounds for charity by climbing the highest mountains in each of the four UK countries. This is what they have to scale:

Country	Mountain	Range	Height
Scotland	Ben Nevis	The Cairngorms	1,344m
Wales	Snowdon	Snowdonia	1,085m
England	Scafell Pike	The Cumbrian Mountains	977m
N Ireland	Slieve Donard	The Mourne Mountains	852m

YOU DON'T NEED SHEEP TO BE A SHEPHERD

The comedian Max Bygraves once noted that when his family came down to London they struggled because his dad couldn't get any work. He was a shepherd. Nice gag, but there was one shepherd that did very well all round London in the early nineteenth century – the engraver Thomas Shepherd. From Regent's Park to St James' Street, Piccadilly to Limehouse, Shepherd recorded through his work a host of landmark sights and views of the time. Having done so, he then went on to compile a catalogue of views of Edinburgh, Bath and Bristol to boot. Some of his images show the still rural nature in the 1820s of parts of London, such as his engraving of St John's Church, Holloway, its wooden fence and arboreal background giving it a distinctly rustic look.

And talking of churches, we're back to Bygraves again...

COUNTRY CONTEMPLATIONS

It is a lovely day during the last week in May. There has been no rain for more than a fortnight; the wind is north-east, and the sun shines brightly, yet we walk down to the River Coln, anticipating a good day's sport among the trout: for, during the may-fly season, no matter how unpropitious the weather may appear, sport is more of a certainty on this stream than at any other time of year. Early in the season drought does not appear to have any effect on the springs; we might get no rain from the middle of April until half-way through June, and yet the water will keep up and remain a good colour all the time. But after June is 'out', down goes the water, lower and lower every week; no amount of rain will then make any perceptible increase to the volume of the stream, and not until the nights begin to lengthen out and the autumnal gales have done their work will the water rise again to its normal height. If you ask Tom Peregrine why these things are so, he will only tell you that after a few gales the 'springs be frum'. The word 'frum', the derivation of which is, Anglo-Saxon, 'fram', or 'from' = strong, flourishing, is the local expression for the bursting of the springs.

Our friend Tom Peregrine is full of these quaint expressions. When he sees a covey of partridges dusting themselves in the roads, he will tell you they are 'bathering'. A dog hunting through a wood is always said to be 'breveting'... The ground on a frosty morning 'scrumps' or feels 'scrumpety' as you walk across the fields; and the partridges when wild are 'teert'. All these phrases are very happy, the sound of the words illustrating exactly the idea they are intended to convey.

J Arthur Gibbs
A Cotswold Village, 1898

George misjudged the jump and landed on his ass.

COUNTRY CONUNDRUMS

A cryptic clue:
Sid enters crop to follow the foreign earl, and make this book (11)
Answer on page 153.

SKIMMING THE SURFACE

Next time you come across a flat lake, and fancy skimming stones across it, here's what you do. According to a team of scientists, the magic angle at which the flat stone should strike the surface of the lake is 20°. Hit that angle, and you've got the best chance of breaking the world record. Good luck, though: it currently stands at 38 skims.

I felt the challenge of those big pines, and became a more competent tree-climber with practice. Getting started up the bare trunk was the usual problem, but the higher one went the safer the climb became. I learned that small and dead snags could often be quite strong, to pull up by and stand on, provided you exerted minimum leverage and kept one arm round the trunk. Larches were treacherous, though, and even quite thick dead branches could snap like carrots, whereas spruce snags often seemed as though made of steel. The pines had a marvellous resinous smell, and the young flaky bark of the upper tree glowed warm russet in the sunlight.

D A Ratcliffe, *In Search of Nature*

WHAT'S IN A NAME: C

Carder	Wool comber
Chandler	Trader or maker of candles
Chevener	Fine stocking maker
Chingler	Roof tiler
Clower	Shoe or nail maker
Cooper	Barrel maker or repairer
Cotter	Agricultural labourer
Crocker	Potter
Currier	Horse dresser or leather tanner
Cutler	Knife maker or seller

THE FOREST FIGHTS BACK

The New Forest is no such thing. It is neither new (it was created by William the Conqueror in the eleventh century), nor is it a forest as we know the term today. In Norman England a forest was an area of land outside usual jurisdiction, giving the king the right to do pretty much whatever he pleased with it. What pleased William was to dispose of the various settlements, farms and villages in that area of Hampshire, and stock the land with deer. If there was anything William liked it was a good hunt. As one twelfth century chronicler,

Orderic Vitalis, wrote: 'So great was his love of woods that he laid waste more than 60 parishes, forced the peasants to move to other places, and replaced the men with beasts of the forest so that he might hunt to his heart's content'.

If anyone was looking to get revenge for this deed, it came in the most ironic of ways. William's second son, Richard, was killed in a hunting accident in the forest, as was his third son, William Rufus, and his grandson, another Richard. The sins of the fathers…

THE COUNTRYSIDE CODE

Most know it exists, few know what it is. A number of different codes have existed in various forms since the 1930s, and were first pulled into some sort of shape in the 1950s soon after the introduction of National Parks. In 1981 the *Country Code* was formalised by the Countryside Commission into a dozen simple points, which included 'Enjoy the countryside and respect its life and work', 'Take your litter home', and 'Make no unnecessary noise'. The trouble was that the code was established to help townies understand what they should and shouldn't do on their visits to rural areas, but made little reference to what those who already lived there should do.

So, in 2004, the government published a new *Countryside Code* for all, which reflected the changes of the previous couple of decades, and in particular the new right of access to open country and registered common land. A concise version of the code is:

Advice for the public

- Be safe – plan ahead and follow any signs.
- Leave gates and property as you find them.
- Protect plants and animals, and take your litter home.
- Keep dogs under close control.
- Consider other people.

Advice for land managers

- Know your rights, responsibilities and liabilities.
- Where can people go on your land?
- What rules apply to people while they are on your land?
- What are your rights and responsibilities towards people on your land?
- Make it easy for visitors to act responsibly.
- How can you help people get access to your land responsibly, and keep to the Countryside Code?
- What help and advice can you get?
- Identify possible threats to visitors' safety.
- Are there any risks to the safety of people on your land, and how can you deal with these risks?

THE LONGEST COUNTRY LANE IN ENGLAND

This was the name once given to the A38, which runs all the way from Bodmin to Mansfield. Much of the route is rural, but for many years, much of it was also covered in cars, it being the main holiday route to the Southwest from the Midlands. The building of the M5 alleviated some of the traffic, making it reasonably quiet – or, at least, as quiet as the longest double-digit A-road in Britain can be.

In 2002, Plantlife International launched a nationwide search for the favourite wild flowers of each county and island. Among the surprises were that, although Lancashire voted for the red rose, Yorkshire went for the harebell. The rest were as follows:

Bedfordshire	*Bee orchid*
Berkshire	*Summer snowflake*
Buckinghamshire	*Chiltern gentian*
Cambridgeshire	*Pasqueflower*
Cheshire	*Cuckooflower*
Cornwall	*Cornish heath*
Cumberland	*Grass-of-Parnassus*
Derbyshire	*Jacob's ladder*
Devon	*Primrose*
Dorset	*Dorset heath*
Durham	*Spring gentian*
Essex	*Poppy*
Gloucestershire	*Wild daffodil*
Hampshire	*Dog-rose*
Herefordshire	*Mistletoe*
Hertfordshire	*Pasqueflower*
Huntingdonshire	*Water-violet*
Isle of Man	*Fuchsia*
Isle of Wight	*Pyramidal orchid*
Isles of Scilly	*Thrift*
Kent	*Hop*
Lancashire	*Red rose*
Leicestershire	*Foxglove*
Lincolnshire	*Common dog-violet*
Middlesex	*Wood anemone*
Norfolk	*Poppy*
Northamptonshire	*Cowslip*
Northumberland	*Bloody crane's-bill*
Nottinghamshire	*Autumn crocus*
Oxfordshire	*Fritillary*
Rutland	*Clustered bellflower*
Shropshire	*Round-leaved sundew*
Somerset	*Cheddar pink*
Staffordshire	*Heather*
Suffolk	*Oxlip*
Surrey	*Cowslip*
Sussex	*Round-headed rampion*
Warwickshire	*Honeysuckle*
Westmorland	*Alpine forget-me-not*
Wiltshire	*Burnt orchid*

36 *Year, in the nineteenth century, of the founding of the Botanical Society of the British Isles*

COBBETT'S CRABBY GOBBETS

William Cobbett, in his visits to the countryside in the early nineteenth century, was not always impressed with what he saw...

A route, when it lies through villages, is one thing on a map, and quite another thing on the ground. Our line of villages from Cheltenham to Fairford was very nearly straight upon the map; but upon the ground it took us round about a great many miles, besides now and then a little going back, to get into the right road; and, which was a great inconvenience, not a public-house was there on our road until we got within eight miles of Fairford. Resolved that not one single farthing of my money should be spent in the Wen of Cheltenham, we came through that place, expecting to find a public-house in the first or second of the villages; but not one was there over the whole of the wold; and though I had, by pocketing some slices of meat and bread at Ryall, provided against this contingency, as far as related to ourselves, I could make no such provision for our horses, and they went a great deal too far without baiting. Plenty of farm-houses, and, if they had been in America, we need have looked for no other. Very likely (I hope it at any rate) almost any farmer on the Cotswold would have given us what we wanted, if we had asked for it; but the fashion, the good old fashion, was, by the hellish system of funding and taxing and monopolising, driven across the Atlantic. And is England never to see it return! Is the hellish system to last for ever!

William Cobbett, *Rural Rides,*
30 September 1826

QUOTE UNQUOTE

New Zealand is not a small country but a large village.
Peter Jackson, director of *The Lord of the Rings*

A SHEEPDOG TRIAL IN SEVEN EASY STEPS

Outrun	When you send the dog away to the sheep.
Lift	The dog begins to move the sheep.
Fetch	The dog brings the sheep to you via the fetch gates.
Drive	Having completed the fetch and driven the sheep around behind you, the dog drives them around the course.
Crossdrive	The dog drives the sheep across the course from the first to the second drive gates.
Shed	You sort out the sheep at the shedding ring, separating some off.
Pen	The enclosure into which the sheep are driven.

Elep-hunting.

COUNTRY CONUNDRUMS

This is an anagram of which countryside writer?
JIM RATES HERO
Answer on page 153.

LAST CHANCE TO SEE

The Lincoln red, one of Britain's rarest cattle breeds, is an example of the decline in the mid-twentieth century of dual-purpose cattle. Bred for both meat and milk, and developed from Shorthorn cattle to be able to handle the cold marshland of Lincolnshire, it became less popular after the war as farmers diversified less, concentrating more on either beef or dairy. This much exported breed, first logged back in 1822, has been introduced into many countries, including USA, Germany, Hungary and New Zealand. Large and fleshy, and cherry red in colour, it's now largely used as a beef breed, and its pure breed numbers have greatly dwindled in recent decades. A survey in 1997 revealed that only 750 breeding females remained.

CROP ROTATION FOR MODERN
SMALL-HOLDERS

The **HENRY DOUBLEDAY RESEARCH ASSOCIATION**, Europe's largest organic membership organisation, has the following advice on rotation planting:

In gardening books it tends to be based on standard British crops – brassicas, legumes, potatoes and so on. Even if you don't grow any of these, you can still devise an effective rotation that suits you and your crops. The usual length is three or four years – crops therefore return to their original site after this time. If the soil is already infected with persistent problems such as eelworm or clubroot, try to extend the rotation of susceptible crops even further.

- List all the veg you want to grow over a season, and the relative quantities of each. Remember to include green manures.

- Group plants together by botanical family. Some relationships may seem a little unlikely, but if you were to let all the plants flower, their family likeness would soon become clear.

- Draw a plan of the growing area. Divide it into equal sized sections according to the number of years you want the rotation to last – try three or four to start with. A 'section' may be made up of several discrete areas, or you may have several 'sections' in a large bed. Distribute your crops within these sections.

- The first rule is to keep families together; if a section is to hold more than one family, try and keep those with similar growing requirements together. Using a bed system can make planning a rotation easier. You may also find it helpful to write crops on to pieces of those moveable sticky note pads. You can then play around until you find a combination that fits.

- You may find, for example, that the quantity of potatoes you had planned, might be too large to fit a section. In this case, reduce the number of plants rather than abandoning the rotation.

- Short term crops such as lettuce and other salads, early carrots and beet can be fitted in on any plot.

- Keep records – of what actually happened, not just what you planned! Use this information when planning next year's cropping.

www.hdra.org.uk

A HELPING HAND

Champions of the countryside in their own words:

The **WILDLIFE TRUSTS** is a partnership of 47 local Wildlife Trusts across the UK, plus the Isle of Man and Alderney.

Our vision is 'an environment richer in wildlife for everyone' and we're the largest UK charity exclusively dedicated to conserving all our habitats and species, with a membership of more than 530,000 people including 62,000 junior members. We campaign for the protection of wildlife and invest in the future by helping people of all ages to gain a greater appreciation and understanding of wildlife. Collectively, we also manage more than 2,500 nature reserves spanning over 80,000 hectares. The Wildlife Trusts also lobby for better protection of the UK's natural heritage and are dedicated to protecting wildlife for the future.

The Wildlife Trusts and their junior branch, Wildlife Watch, work together to protect wildlife in towns and the countryside.

www.wildlifetrusts.org

QUOTE UNQUOTE

If you tell a joke in the forest, but nobody laughs, was it a joke?
Steven Wright, US comedian

FIELD FARE

Birds on the British list named after their dinners:
Sparrowhawk
Kingfisher
Spotted and pied flycatchers
Linnet (named after the Latin for flax, *lin*)
European bee-eater
And one that fortunately isn't: cattle egret

COUNTRY CONTEMPLATIONS

There is a rhythm about country paths that can be quickly felt by those who walk along them. I would go so far as to say that I know instinctively the way a path must run. Up beside the hedge, over a stile, across a field, and straight on through woods to a swing-gate; and on and on and on again, through the villages, stretching, as it were, into infinity.
I know nothing about roads, except the ones that are really ancient tracks in a new guise; but I never weary of the fieldpaths, and as I walk along them, I feel in tune with the good earth that is my heritage.
Henry Fearon, *Mark My Footsteps*

WORKING DOGS

Terriers

Sir Walter Scott was one of the first to write about fox-hunting terriers as a specific breed, his novel *Guy Mannering* describing them as 'mustards and peppers'. They soon picked up a new name however, taken from one of the characters in the book – Dandie Dinmont. Over in England, meanwhile, some of the early mounted hunts that grew out of the Enclosures Act which forced the poor off the land, were organised by a reverend who used to bring his terrier with him. He soon discovered that the terrier was a ferocious little hunter in its own right, and the realisation that terriers made good fox-hunters, thanks to their ability to dash into tunnels and their tenacious nature, began to dawn.

That reverend's name? John, or Jack, Russell.

THERE'S SOMETHING VAGUELY FAMILIAR ABOUT THIS BOOK

- *The Countryside Companion*, by Janet Trewin, was published in 1996
- *The Countryside Companion*, by Sam Elder, was published in 1995
- *Larousse Countryside Companion*, by Michael Chinery, was published in 1995
- *The Countryside Companion*, by Geoffrey Young, was published in 1993
- *Countryside Companion*, by David Parry and John Oliver, was published in 1993
- *The Countryside Companion*, by Godfrey Cave, was published in 1992
- *The Countryside Companion*, by Wynford Vaughan-Thomas, was published in 1980

THE GOLDEN RURAL

Rural and rustic should really both mean the same thing, each derived from the Latin 'rus', meaning open land or country. Around 1550, however, the two terms began to diverge in meaning. Get the wrong one today, and you might well offend. The *Oxford English Dictionary* explains it best: 'In early examples, there is usually little or no difference between the meanings of rural and rustic, but in later use the tendency is to employ rural when the idea of locality (country scenes, etc) is prominent, and rustic when there is a suggestion of the more primitive qualities or manners naturally attaching to country life.'

OH DEAR ODONATA

Forty years ago, the UK boasted 42 breeding species of dragonfly... but no longer. Three of these have become extinct in the country already: the orange-spotted emerald was lost when a sewage spillage resulted in the pollution of its last remaining breeding ground; the Norfolk damselfly was unable to survive the pollution of sites where it had previously thrived; and the dainty damselfly was eliminated when flooding destroyed its Essex habitat.

The British Dragonfly Society (www.dragonflysoc.org.uk) has drawn up a list of ways that our remaining species can be protected and encouraged:

- Dig small ponds in gardens and larger ones in various types of open space. It will not be long before dragonflies start to colonise them, since most species readily discover new habitats.
- Urge farmers and other land-owners to preserve their hedgerows and copses, where adult dragonflies shelter in dull weather, and to keep ponds and other water on their land clear of effluents.
- Lakes and ponds should not be allowed to become overgrown with reeds and other aquatic plants (though they should not be totally denuded of them), nor should the branches of over-hanging trees be permitted to block out the sun.
- Take special precautions against polluting the water when holidaying in such places as the Norfolk Broads.
- Refrain from taking specimens unnecessarily; photographs generally provide a satisfactory means of identifying species and provide excellent records.

PLENTY OF ROOM ON TOP

There's nothing particularly new about treehouses – old engravings from the South Pacific show images of people living in thatched nests, riding up and down to their homes in baskets. The thing is, not many of the really old ones are still around. In a corner of Shropshire, however, still stands – or perches – possibly the oldest extant treehouse in the world. Built in 1692 in a lime tree in the grounds of Pitchford Hall, near Shrewsbury, it contains gothic windows and an oak floor, and is in the style of the Hall itself.

It's had its share of famous visitors too. In 1832, a 13 year-old girl visited and recorded the occasion in her journal: 'At a little past one we came home and walked about the grounds, and I went up a staircase to a little house in a tree'. Five years later, that young girl became Queen Victoria.

NOW LOOK, I SAY, JUST LOOKIE HERE

At last: a complete list of all 28 *Looney Tunes* starring Foghorn Leghorn, the best rooster ever to strut the silver screen:

Walky Talky Hawky	*All Fowled Up*
Crowing Pains	*Weasel Stop*
The Foghorn Leghorn	*The High and the Flighty*
Henhouse Henery	*Raw! Raw! Rooster*
The Leghorn Blows at Midnight	*Fox Terror*
A Fractured Leghorn	*Feather Bluster*
Leghorn Swoggled	*Weasel While you Work*
Lovelorn Leghorn	*A Broken Leghorn*
Sock-a-Doodle-Do	*Crockett-Doodle-Do*
The Egg-cited Rooster	*The Dixie Fryer*
Plop Goes the Weasel	*Strangled Eggs*
Of Rice and Hen	*The Slick Chick*
Little Boy Boo	*Mother Was a Rooster*
Feather Dusted	*Banty Raids*

COUNTRY CONUNDRUMS

A cryptic clue:
Babbling novel about first republic (5)
Answer on page 153.

FUNNY FARM

A farmer comes home from the fields one day and notices that his barn is on fire. Frantically, he dashes into the house and calls the local village fire brigade, who set off at high speed. Anxiously watching from the safety of the lane, the farmer sees the fire engine coming and watches aghast as it swings into his farm and drives straight through the flames into the middle of the barn. Through the flames he can just make out the firemen as they jump out of the engine and begin spraying water all around them: it's an astonishing effort, and the blaze is put out in minutes. The farmer dashes up to the fire chief: 'That was one of the bravest things I've ever seen', he gushes. 'You actually put that fire out from its centre. Stunning. Here, let me give you this.' And so great is his admiration and gratitude he writes out a cheque for £500 on the spot and hands it over.

A few minutes later they're all sitting in the farm kitchen having a relaxing cup of tea. 'So, what do you think you'll spend that money on?' asks the farmer.

The fire chief doesn't hesitate. 'Some new brakes for the fire engine for starters.'

Terms you won't hear so much now that hunting with hounds has been banned in Britain, (that doesn't mean they won't exist – just that you won't hear them so much):

Couple	A pair of hounds: they're always counted in couples
Covert	A small area of woodland where foxes hide
Draw	Send in the hounds to flush out the fox
Give tongue	The yowl of a hound on picking up the scent of a fox
Lodge	The hounds' home
Music	When the hounds give tongue
Whipper in	Assistant to the huntsman
Work a line	Follow a scent trail

QUOTE UNQUOTE

*Few things are more pleasant than a village graced with
a good church, a good priest and a good pub.*
John Hillaby, travel writer

A HELPING HAND

Champions of the countryside in their own words:

The **ROYAL SOCIETY FOR THE PROTECTION OF BIRDS (RSPB)** stands for birds, for people, for ever. We've all seen astonishing changes in our daily lives, and our birds and other wildlife are struggling to keep their place in this fast-changing world. The RSPB works throughout the UK, developing practical conservation solutions that put birds back into the picture and safe-guard their futures.

With the support of our members and a caring public, the RSPB is tackling bird declines head on. For instance, we:

- Develop and manage over 100 nature reserves around the UK, where you can see birds in the wild, busily getting on with their everyday lives.
- Work with government, industry, farmers and developers to put the needs of birds firmly into the debate and to influence decisions and actions.
- Carry out essential research so that we fully understand why some bird species – like the song thrush and house sparrow – are declining, and how we can help bring these birds back from the brink.
- Work outside the UK, to shape and influence what happens to UK birds on migration, and to other wild birds around the globe.

www.rspb.org.uk

FIRST OF THE SUMMER WINE

When fans first heard and saw their favourite rural fictional shows:

The Archers, 1 January 1951 (a pilot was broadcast in 1950)
Emmerdale Farm, 16 September 1972
Last of the Summer Wine, 4 January 1973
Heartbeat, 10 April 1992
Monarch of the Glen, 27 February 2000

COUNTRY CONTEMPLATIONS

I went into the oak wood one morning, and... here I found a dead squirrel lying on the turf under one of the biggest oaks, looking exceedingly conspicuous with the bright morning sun shining on him. Looking closely at my dead squirrel to make sure that he had no external hurt, I was surprised to find its fur peopled with lively black fleas, running about as if very much upset at the death of their host. These fleas were to my eyes just like *pulex irritans* – our own flea; but it is doubtful that it was the same, as we know that a great many animals have their own species to tease them. Now, I have noticed that some very small animals have very small fleas; and that, one would imagine, is as it should be, since fleas are small to begin with, because they cannot afford to be large, and the flea that would be safe on a dog would be an unsuitable parasite for so small a creature as a mouse.

The common shrew is an example. It has often happened that when in an early morning walk I have found one lying dead on the path or road and have touched it, out instantly a number of fleas have jumped. And on touching it again, there may be a second and third shower. These fleas, parasitical on so minute a mammal, are themselves minute – pretty sherry-coloured little creatures, not half so big as the dog's flea. It appears to be a habit of some wild fleas, when the animal they live on dies and grows cold, to place themselves on the surface of the fur and to hop well away when shaken. But we do not yet know very much about their lives. Huxley once said that we were in danger of being buried under our accumulated monographs. There is, one is sorry to find, no monograph on the fleas; a strange omission, when we consider that we have, as the lifework of an industrious German, a big handsome quarto, abundantly illustrated, on the more degraded and less interesting *Pedicularia*.

W H Hudson,
Hampshire Days.
This book was written in 1903, a few years before Miriam Rothschild, botanist, lepidopterist, and monograph writer on fleas, was born. The 'Pedicularia' that Hudson was so disparaging about are cowries.

THE ANCIENT YEAR

The Pagan seasonal cycle is often called the 'Wheel of the Year' and contains eight major festivals fairly evenly spaced, like spokes in a wheel:

Samhain/Halloween (31 October) – a time to honour the ancestors, and prepare for the depths of winter. The God enters the underworld, symbolically dying so that the earth and life may continue.

Yule/Midwinter (21-22 December) – a time to celebrate the longest night with feasting and merriment, and the rebirth of the God.

Imbolc (Beginning of February) – the beginning of Spring, lengthening days and the return of warmth and life. The Goddess, represented by nature, begins to awake from her winter's slumber.

Spring Equinox/Ostara (21-22 March) – the lighter half of the year begins. The God, represented by the Sun, begins to gain in strength.

Beltane (Beginning of May) – the start of Summer, a time to rejoice and make merry. Throughout the country villages celebrate with Green Men, morris dancing and maypoles.

Summer Solstice (21-22 June) – the longest day, when the God is at the peak of his strength.

Lammas (Beginning of August) – the celebration of the first harvest from the fields, when the corn is cut and winter looms.

Autumnal Equinox (21-22 September) – the darker half of the year begins, and the God is on the wane, readying for his descent into the kingdom of death.

SINGS OF A DOVE

There's a pigeon-like bird sitting up in the tree, but you're not sure which species it is. Perhaps its call will help. The woodpigeon coos a five-note call, 'hoo-HOO-hoo hoo hoo', the last two notes falling away, while the stock dove utters more of a growling sound: 'ooo-uuu-ohh'. The collared dove, a recent addition to Britain's avifauna having arrived only in the 1950s, emits the already familiar 'hoo HOOOO hu', while its close relative, the summer-visiting turtle dove purrs out a gentle 'turr turr turr', from which it gets its name. Should you be near the coast, you may hear the call of the rock dove, a bubbling gurgle that would sound rather strange if it were not for the fact that we've become quite familiar with the sound from the many feral pigeons of towns and cities, most of which were descended from this species.

STAG FRIGHT

It was only a couple of decades ago that a wander at dusk in June through woods, fields, and even gardens, could put you in great danger. It would begin with a low humming sound, develop into a rattling raspberry, and conclude with a thump to the side of your head. Well, perhaps thump is too strong a word – a 'toc' to the side of the head is probably more accurate. It was a male stag beetle, buzzing steadily around hunting for a female, colliding with anything that its headlong flight rendered it incapable of manoeuvring around.

Such impressive brushes with nature are, sadly, rare these days. Stag beetles are on the decline, because the decaying wood they need to lay their eggs in is rapidly being cleared up in the woodlands, hedgerows and gardens of the south where they used in particular to be reasonably abundant.

There's an easy way of bringing them back, though: just leave dead wood lying around the place, and perhaps one day the sight of people ducking their heads on a warm summer's evening will return.

SOME CINEMATIC TREE-TS

Hearts of Oak, 1924
Nightmare on Elm Street, 1984
Birch Interval, 1977
Willow, 1988
Ash Wednesday, 1973
Cypress Edge, 1999
The Trail of the Lonesome Pine, 1936
Soul Plane, 2004
FIR, 1999

COUNTRY CONTEMPLATIONS

When I was a lad, there used to be a gang of poachers in our village; they went out at night as regularly in the seasons as others went to their day's work and their harvesting. There were, I believe, four or five, or maybe more, of them. The gang broke up some years ago. One or two are still alive, and following constant work; the others are old, or dead. A professional or gang-poacher generally gave it up when he was about fifty or so, because he began then to get stiff, and lost his speed. Poaching means very quick work, and, to succeed at it, a man is bound to be a fast runner, agile, and quick-witted.

Between Earth and Sky, 1898.
Joseph Arch: the story of his life, as told by himself

So, you're out walking on some common land, and you sit down for a cheese sandwich and a packet of crisps. You look down at your feet and see that the earth's been scuffed up a bit and... is that something gleaming out at you? With a history like Britain's there's buried treasure all over the land – coins, artefacts – and even if you're not looking for it, you might stumble across something. The question is, what do you do with it? Under the Treasure Act of 1996, you now have to report it to the coroner to the county archaeologist within 14 days of realising that it might be treasure. The next question is: what qualifies? The following should help:

The following finds are treasure under the Act:

Objects other than coins: any object other than a coin provided that it contains at least 10 per cent of gold or silver and is at least 300 years old when found.

Coins: all coins from the same find provided that there are at least two and they are at least 300 years old when found (but if the coins contain less than 10 per cent of gold or silver there must be at least 10 of them).

An object or coin is part of the same find as another object or coin if it is found in the same place as, or had previously been left together with, the other object. Finds may have become scattered since they were originally deposited in the ground.

Only the following groups of coins will normally be regarded as coming form the 'same find':
(a) hoards that have been deliberately hidden;
(b) smaller groups of coins, such as the contents of purses, that may have been dropped or lost;
(c) and votive or ritual deposits.

Single coins found on their own are not treasure regardless of material, and groups of coins lost one by one over a period of time (for example those found on settlement sites or on fair sites) will not normally be treasure.

Associated objects: any object, whatever it is made of, that is found in the same place as, or had previously been together with, another object that is treasure.

Objects that would have been treasure trove: any object that would previously have been treasure trove, but does not fall within the specific categories given above. These objects have to be made substantially of gold or silver; they have to have been buried with the intention of recovery and their owner or his heirs cannot be traced.

The following types of find are not treasure:

Those objects whose owners can be traced.

Unworked natural objects: including human and animal remains, even if they are found in association with treasure.

Objects from the foreshore: if there is evidence that they have come from a wreck.

This plant is out of selfish, endless zeal (8)

Answer on page 153.

QUOTE UNQUOTE

*Many of our own people here in this country do not
ask about computers, telephones and television sets.
They ask – when will we get a road to our village.*
Thabo Mbeki, President of South Africa

WHAT'S IN A NAME: F

Faber	Artisan
Fagetter	Firewood seller
Fanner	Grain winnower
Farrier	Blacksmith who shoes horses
Faulkner	Falconer
Ferreter	Maker of silk tape
Fettler	Cleaner of mill machinery
Fletcher	Arrow maker
Fuller	Cloth cleaner

HOW TO MAKE A DAISY CHAIN

- First, grow a long thumbnail. Once you're so equipped, find yourself a field full of daisies, and bring your thumbnail with you.
- Pick the daisies with the longest stalks, and with your nail, pierce a small slot in the first daisy's stalk.
- Thread the second daisy through that slot, and pierce its stalk, making a new slot.
- Thread the third daisy through that slot, and pierce its stalk, making a new slot.
- Thread the fourth daisy through that slot, and pierce its stalk, making a new slot.
- Thread the fifth daisy through that slot, and pierce its stalk, making a new slot.
- If you haven't got the idea by now, best to get back home and just watch some TV. You're rubbish.

QUOTE UNQUOTE

*To forget how to dig the earth and to tend
the soil is to forget ourselves.*
Mohandas 'Mahatma' Gandhi, Indian statesman

PLEASE FLY AWAY HOME

There's a predator rampaging the British countryside, destroying the locals and the life that supports them, and doing it very quickly too. No need to lock your doors, though: this particular beast is a ladybird.

The harlequin ladybird was first spotted in Britain in 2004, brought in accidentally on imported plants, and it spread its range very rapidly. The trouble is that it not only more efficiently devours the aphids that our native ladybirds require... it eats the ladybirds too! And if it's still hungry, butterfly eggs, caterpillars and lacewing larvae can also turn up on the menu.

So how do you spot a harlequin? Unfortunately, they come in various forms. They tend to be a little rounder than our native species, and about the same size as the common seven-spot, but their colours can vary. They can be black with two or four orange or red spots, or orange with between 15 and 20 black spots. The main marker, however, is the white plate behind the back of its head which has a big, black M-shaped marking upon it... apart from on some of the black versions.

Confused? To find out more, visit www.harlequin-survey.org, set up by the National History Museum, The Wildlife Trusts and others to monitor the insect's devastating progress across the countryside.

LIGHT IN APRIL

The novelist William Faulkner was quite the romantic at heart. On one occasion, having met a woman that he wanted to get to know better, he invited her to see what he considered one of the most beautiful of sights: a young bride in her wedding dress. The companion agreed, and they set off in his car down the back roads, finally turning into a meadow, whereupon Faulkner turned off his lights and crawled slowly along.

Finally, they reached their destination, and he stopped the car, telling his friend that the bride was standing right in front of them. Then he turned on his headlights to reveal... an apple tree resplendent in its springtime blossom.

D IS FOR DEVONIAN DIALECT, AND...

Daychin'	Thatching
Deesh washer	Wagtail
Dew snail	Slug
Dimpsy	Twilight
Donnikin	Outdoor toilet
Dreckly	Later
Drexil	Doorstep
Dowel	The Devil
Dumble drane	Bumblebee

WORKING DOGS

Labradors and retrievers

In the early hunting days, many breeds of dogs, as well as mongrels, were known as retrievers simply for the reason that they fetched the kill. By the mid-nineteenth century, however, as hunting increased and rapid-loading of guns improved a hunter's daily haul, much of the kill was being lost or left behind, as retrieving was a secondary skill in many breeds. In the 1870s, however, a certain breed of dog from Newfoundland started to appear in Britain, imported for its hunting skills. The labrador was known across the pond for its extreme loyalty and companionship to the fishermen of the islands, and this devotion, matched with keen senses, made it an ideal retriever.

In Scotland, meanwhile, Lord Tweedmouth of Inverness was experimenting with various breeds to discover the ideal dog for retrieving wildfowl. He finally hit upon a mix of water spaniel, setter and foxhound, which produced a line of beautiful yellow dogs with an enthusiastic nature: the golden retriever was born.

I SAID SUFFIX, NOT SUSSEX

How to date a village by its last few letters:

Early Anglo-Saxon	*-hamstede, -ham, -hamsteall, -hamtun, -ingas, -ingham*
Intermediate Anglo-Saxon	*-tun*
Late Anglo-Saxon	*-wic, -cot, -worth, -leah, -feld*
Scandinavian	*-thorp, -by*

COUNTRY CONTEMPLATIONS

The shepherds idle hours are over now
Nor longer leaves him neath the hedgrow bough
On shadow pillowd banks and lolling stile
Wilds looses now their summer friends awhile
Shrill whistles barking dogs and chiding scold
Drive bleating sheep each morn from fallow fold
To wash pits where the willow shadows lean
Dashing them in their fold staind coats to clean
Then turnd on sunning sward to dry agen
They drove them homeward to the clipping pen
In hurdles pent where elm or sycamore
Shut out the sun – or in some threshing floor
There they wi scraps of songs and laugh and tale
Lighten their anual toils while merry ale
Goes round and gladdens old mens hearts to praise
The thread bare customs of old farmers days

John Clare,
The Shepherds Calendar – June
(With a deliberate lack of use of punctuation for effect.)

YOUTH HOSPITABLE ASSOCIATION

If the term eco-friendly had existed back in the 1930s, it would most probably have been applied to the Youth Hostels Association, which was founded partly to encourage young people to look after themselves and find out more about the world around them at the same time. Well, times have moved on, and in 2005 the YHA has now launched the first official eco-friendly youth hostel. Based in Lockton in North Yorkshire, the hostel boasts showers heated by solar panels, a dry compost toilet, and a system that harvests rainwater to use for flushing toilets. The building itself is insulated with sheep's wool, and a new extension has a living sedum roof, which will provide a habitat for wildlife.

A new type of hostel to deal with a hostile world.

Champions of the countryside in their own words:

BUTTERFLY CONSERVATION maintains that if you had been alive a hundred years ago, and went for a summer's walk in the countryside, you would have expected to see a wealth of butterflies.

Today, their numbers have declined seriously and five of our 59 resident species have become extinct. The future of nearly half our remaining species hangs in the balance as they continue to decline in many areas. Moths (the largely nocturnal cousins of butterflies) have also disappeared at an alarming rate and over 50 of our 900 larger species are now highly threatened.

The intensification of farming and forestry have led to widespread destruction of flower-rich meadows, hedgerows, ancient woodland and wild corners – all crucial habitats for butterflies and other wildlife. Wild areas have also been lost to housing and roads, and many remaining fragments are deteriorating due to neglect. Our native deciduous woodlands, home to many of our more sensitive butterflies, have also changed out of all recognition and have either become too shady for butterflies or replaced with dense conifer plantations.

It may be impossible to put the clock back completely but much can be done to increase butterflies and moths and save threatened species from extinction. This is the aim of Butterfly Conservation, but we need your help to achieve it.

www.butterfly-conservation.org

TONIGHT, JOSEF STALIN WILL BE PLAYED BY...

The generally accepted personifications (or animalifications, rather) of leaders, social groups and concepts of Soviet Russia in George Orwell's *Animal Farm*:

Napoleon	Stalin
Snowball	Trotsky
Old Major	Marx – although some compare him to Lenin
Jones the farmer	Tsar Nicholas
Boxer	The Soviet working class
Squealer	The Soviet propaganda machine
Dogs	The Red Army
Mollie	The Russian emigre community
Moses	Christianity, or Western opinion
Frederick	Hitler

Acre.

COUNTRY CONUNDRUMS

I'M IN MOTH, FERRET, VENISON, TERN
Fine. So what's your job?
Answer on page 153.

LAST CHANCE TO SEE

An alert and active breed, the Hackney horse is still alive and well as a show breed, but its traditional role in English society is long gone. Deriving its name from the French 'haquenee', meaning an ambling horse, the Hackney's character and propensity to trot made it an ideal horse for hire, and by the seventeenth century Pepys was using the word to describe horse-drawn carriages for hire. The Hackney cab became a familiar urban sight, the breed itself still being used in the first world war as an artillery horse and even sometimes for cavalry purposes. As the century wore on, however, it soon became redundant as the engine took over. The surviving thousand or so individuals can now be seen in competitions up and down the country, and are sometimes used as crosses to breed show jumpers.

The clearest way into the Universe is through a forest wilderness.
John Muir, naturalist

WREKIN HAVOC

An old folktale explaining the true origin of the Wrekin, the 1,334 foot high hill standing on the Shropshire plain:

There was once a wicked old giant in Wales, who had been banished there by the people of Salisbury and had developed a very great spite against them. As the years passed since his banishment, he steadily planned his revenge, and finally came up with an idea: he would dam the Severn, and cause such a flood that the town would be drowned.

So off he set, carrying a mighty spadeful of earth, tramping along mile after mile trying to find his way back to Shrewsbury. But so many years had it been since last he was there, he had forgotten the route. He went some way off course, and found himself eventually at Wellington, tired and confused, and beginning to lose interest in his great plan. He did not realise how close to Shrewsbury he was.

Sitting by the side of the road to get his breath back, he espied a man coming down the road towards him. It was a cobbler with a sack of old boots and shoes strung on his back, who was from Wellington, and who once a fortnight walked to Shrewsbury to collect his customers' old boots and shoes, and take them home with him to mend.

The giant called out to him. 'I say, how far is it to Shrewsbury?'

'Shrewsbury?' replied the cobbler. 'What do you want at Shrewsbury?'

'I want to fill up the Severn with this lump of earth I've got here' he answered. 'I've an old grudge against the mayor and the folks at Shrewsbury, and I mean to drown them and get rid of them all at once.'

The cobbler considered this, and realised it would not do. He could not afford to lose all his customers in this way, so thinking quickly, he undid his sack.

'Look at these' he said to the giant, showing him the old boots he was carrying. 'I've come from Shrewsbury myself, and I've worn these out on my march'.

The giant moaned. 'Oh, then it's no use. I'm exhausted already, and can't carry this load of mine any further.' And so saying, he dropped the earth on the ground just where he stood, scraped his boots with his spade, turned on his heel, and was never seen again.

And where he put down his load stands the Wrekin to this day. And by its side stands the little Ercall, made from the earth he scraped off his boots.

The night was of a Cimmerian blackness. In the tree-tops the wind raved like a demented thing. All round me, as I felt my way along with my feet, a thousand little rivulets splashed and gurgled in the deep of the woods. But I was not long in striking Slumberwell. The lane plunged down into what seemed interminable forest, then brought up short on a spit of grassland, which, next morning, I discovered to be the village-green. Friendly lights beamed out at me from all sides; and as I stopped outside one of the large houses, there sounded overhead a familiar creaking and groaning, which I knew to be an inn-sign battling with the breeze.

That evening I spent by the tap-room fire, in an old oak settle; with the landlord's slippers on my feet; the jovial, white-haired landlord himself at my elbow; the landlady, in curl-papers and spectacles, sewing by the light of a tallow candle hard by; and a wonderful old man and his son, to complete the company. Others dropped in from time to time, and dropped out again; but we five made up the enduring elements of the scene. We took it in turn to keep the talk going, and the process was surprisingly easy. Each in turn related some simple experience, the simpler the better, provided it was wrapped about with numberless little details and unimportant etceteras, and spun out to its last reach. The old ploughman was specially great at this gentle exercise, and held our little circle spell-bound for a whole ten minutes while, for instance, he related how he had succeeded in stopping a pig.

Tickner Edwardes,
Lift-luck on Southern Roads

ARABLE BABBLE

Terms you'll need to know if you want to be a crop farmer:

Awns	The 'hairs' that sprout from ears of corn
Binder	Horse or tractor-drawn tool that cuts cereals and ties them into sheaves
Break crop	A rotational crop that helps replenish the earth
Chits	New growth on plants
Clamp	A mass of fodder crop
Game cover	Seed-bearing plants that provide cover for pheasants and partridges
Ley	Grassed area
Mole plough	A tool that digs deep holes to aid drainage
Rogue	Unwanted plant in crop fields
Stook	Collection of drying sheaves
Tilth	Soil that's been broken down into a fine substance

56 *Percentage of young people in rural areas of Cheshire dissatisfied with the facilities available to them*

28 DAYS LATER

The Archers, that everyday tale of country folk, got some of its days back in 2005. Although the show has been fully archived since 1994, only key episodes were previously kept, leading to whole swathes believed lost. But it turned out that Radio Wiltshire had 28 episodes in a dusty store cupboard, donated to them by a listener who had recorded them all in 1977. Now, some of the classic tales of Ambridge and its inhabitants can be reheard and reheard again, including:

- Shula Archer losing her virginity to the editor of the *Borchester Echo*.
- Walter Gabriel's homelessness.
- Tony Archer trying to secure the tenancy of Bridge Farm.
- Tony's attempts to seduce Libby the milkmaid while his wife is away looking after her sick mother.

Great tales. Great memories.

WHAT'S IN A NAME: H

Hackler	Comber of coarse flax in linen-making
Haywood	Inspector of parish boundaries
Higgler	Peddler
Hillier	Roof tiler
Henter	Thief
Hobbler	Tower of river boats
Hoyman	Coastal ferryman

THE WARHORSE AND THE SHEEP

Winston Churchill, when he wasn't out fighting wars or writing up his nation's history, rather enjoyed painting his favourite countryside views. He wasn't too bad, either, and some of his paintings popped up in various living rooms and halls in both Britain and the US. While visiting Henry Luce, the publisher of *Time* magazine, he spotted one of his landscapes hanging over the mantelpiece, and asked Luce what he thought of it.

'I'm very fond of it,' replied Luce, 'but I can't help feeling that it would have benefited from a bit more life in it, perhaps some sheep in that field, for example.' Churchill grunted and said no more, and Luce was a touch concerned that he might have offended the old bulldog. His concern grew to alarm a few days later when a call from Churchill's office came through, requesting the return of the painting.

Within the week, however, his mind was put at rest. The painting was sent back – with a single sheep added into the foreground.

ASS ME NO QUESTIONS

**The best of the countryside's donkey beliefs,
(one or two are rather asinine):**

- Wear the hairs from a donkey's back in a charm around your neck to guard against whooping-cough and toothache. The dark mark on the animal's spine is said to have appeared after it bore Christ into Jerusalem.
- If your mare is pregnant, set a black donkey into the field with her, and she won't miscarry.
- If you see a dead donkey, good luck will come your way – particularly if you jump over the body three times.
- Having said that, you're unlikely to see one. Donkeys were believed to know when they were about to die, and hide themselves away.
- A braying donkey that twitches its ears foretells rain.
- If your child is sick, ride a donkey backwards, facing the tail end.

QUOTE UNQUOTE

Let anyone who possesses a vivid imagination and a highly-wrought nervous system, even now, in this century, with all the advantages of learning and science, go and sit among the rocks, or in the depths of the wood, and think of immortality, and all that that word really means, and by-and-by a mysterious awe will creep into the mind, and it will half believe in the possibility of seeing or meeting something – something – it knows not exactly what.
Richard Jefferies, nature writer.

COBBETT'S CRABBY GOBBETS

William Cobbett, in his visits to the countryside in the early nineteenth century, was not always impressed with what he saw...

From London to Reigate, through Sutton, is about as villainous a tract as England contains. The soil is a mixture of gravel and clay, with big yellow stones in it, sure sign of really bad land. Before you descend the hill to go into Reigate, you pass Gatton ('Gatton and Old Sarum'), which is a very rascally spot of earth. The trees are here a week later than they are at Tooting. At Reigate they are (in order to save a few hundred yards length of road) cutting through a hill. They have lowered a little hill on the London side of Sutton. Thus is the money of the country actually thrown away: the produce of labour is taken from the industrious, and given to the idlers.

William Cobbett,
Rural Rides, 5 May, 1823

I THINK THAT I SHALL NEVER SEE,
A PROVERB LOVELY AS A TREE

*Around a flowering tree, one
finds many insects.*
Guinean proverb

*Though a tree grows so high, the
falling leaves return to the root.*
Malay proverb

*Keep a green tree in your heart
and perhaps a singing bird
will come.*
Chinese proverb

*From a fallen tree, all make
kindling.*
Spanish proverb

A tree falls the way it leans.
Bulgarian proverb

*A tree does not move unless
there is wind.*
Afghan proverb

*A seed hidden in the heart
of an apple is an orchard
invisible.*
Welsh proverb

*A society grows great when
old men plant trees whose
shade they know they shall
never sit in.*
Greek proverb

*A fool sees not the same tree
that a wise man sees.*
William Blake, *Proverbs of
Hell*, 1790

BRITISH MOTHS WITH IDENTITY CRISES

Common swift
The shark
Reed leopard
Peach blossom
Wood tiger
Dog's tooth
Beaded chestnut

OF FLOCKS AND FLAGONS

The sight of lambs gambolling in the fields is one of the classic countryside images. They look as if they're drunk on the rich new life that Springtime brings. Well, on one farm in 2005, they were. Ordan Vandov, a Macedonian shepherd, had stopped off while herding his flock home to chat to his neighbour who owned a vineyard. The sheep managed to get into some of the pressed grape juice, and when Ordan turned back to them, they were flinging themselves around the yard. Not for long, though. After a few minutes they started swaying and tottering... and Ordan had to borrow a truck to get the drunken flock home. They were completely sheep-faced.

FUNNY FARM

A man is driving down the motorway, outside lane, when he glances into the mirror and sees what looks like a chicken running along behind him. Somewhat startled, he pulls over into the middle lane, the chicken accelerates past, and the driver notices that it's got three legs. Astonished, he gives chase. Eventually, the chicken sticks out a wing, swings across into the inside lane and speeds off the motorway. The man follows it, as it dashes left at the roundabout, sprints off at the second right, and then turns into a country lane and nips around the back of a farm. Pulling up at the farm gate, the man gets out and approaches the farmer.

'Excuse me,' he says, 'this might sound a bit ridiculous, but I'm sure that a three-legged chicken just ran into here.'

'More'n likely,' says the farmer. 'We breed 'em here'.

'Ah,' says the man, feeling somewhat relieved that his eyes hadn't been playing tricks on him. 'Why do you do that, then?'

'Well,' says the farmer, 'I like a leg; the wife, she likes a leg; and the boy, he likes a leg 'n' all.'

'I see, I see. What do they taste like?'

'Dunno. Never caught one.'

COUNTRY CONTEMPLATIONS

Nowhere else does the greater light so rule the day, so measure, so divide, so reign, make so imperial laws, so visibly kindle, so immediately quicken, so suddenly efface, so banish, so restore, as in a plain like this of Suffolk with its enormous sky. The curious have an insufficient motive for going to the mountains if they do it to see the sunrise. The sun that leaps from a mountain peak is a sun past the dew of his birth; he has walked some way towards the common fires of noon. But on the flat country the uprising is early and fresh, the arc is wide, the career is long. The most distant clouds, converging in the beautiful and little-studied order of cloud-perspective (for most painters treat clouds as though they formed perpendicular and not horizontal scenery), are those that gather at the central point of sunrise. On the plain, and there only, can the construction – but that is too little vital a word; I should rather say the organism – the unity, the design of the sky be understood. The light wind that has been moving all night is seen to have not worked at random. It has shepherded some small flocks of cloud afield and folded others. There's husbandry in Heaven. And the order has, or seems to have, the sun for its midst. Not a line, not a curve, but confesses its membership in a design declared from horizon to horizon.

Alice Meynell, *The Rhythm of Life and Other Essays*

HOW TO REACT IF YOU'RE A SHEEPDOG
AND YOU HEAR THESE COMMANDS

Away to me	Move around the sheep in an anti-clockwise direction
Come by	Move around the sheep in a clockwise direction
Get back	Move back and give the sheep room
In here	Move through a gap between sheep to separate them.
Lie down	As well as the obvious, can also mean stand still or slow down
Look back	You've left some sheep behind. Go get 'em
Take time	Slow down
That'll do	Go back to your handler
There	Move straight towards the sheep
Walk Up	As above

Please note that the phrase *'That'll do, pig, that'll do'*, is used only for porcine manoeuvres.

COUNTRY CONUNDRUMS

If you're crossing a field with your boyfriend, which anagrammatised breed below would you not want to meet?
ENDANGERS BEAU
Answer on page 153.

KING ARTHURSKI

The English claim him as their own, as do the Scots and the Welsh. There are some who would have him as Roman. But now there's a theory that Arthur, that great rural king, was in actual fact Russian. The thinking is that the Sarmatians, a nomadic group who made their way from Central Asia to Europe, finally ended up in Britain in the second century as workers for the Romans. A warrior race, skilled with swords and on horseback, they were used to guard Hadrian's Wall, and their tales of derring-do may well have been passed on to the Anglo-Saxons. Intriguingly, there is a race of people today in the Russian Caucasus – the Ossetians – who are descended from the Sarmatians, and who tell tales of a king with a magic sword who followed a chalice of truth. Even the name Excalibur is thought by the same theorists possibly to have derived from a Greek word for a group of famous blacksmiths, the Kalybes, who once lived where the Ossetians live today.

It seems that Arthur, whoever he may have been, is as fascinating a legend today as he ever was.

A HELPING HAND

Champions of the countryside in their own words:

THE RAMBLERS' ASSOCIATION is Britain's biggest charity working to promote walking and to improve conditions for all walkers. With 143,000 members in England, Scotland and Wales, we've been working for walkers for 70 years.

Through our network of dedicated volunteers and staff, we support all who walk, from beginners to experienced enthusiasts, family groups to solitary strollers and the very young to the young at heart.

We are dedicated to:

- Safeguarding Britain's unique network of public paths – all too often, they are illegally blocked, obstructed and overgrown. We work with local authorities to make them a pleasure to walk on
- Providing information to help you plan your walk and enjoy it in safety and comfort
- Increasing access for walkers – our work is helping to establish statutory rights of access to the outdoors
- Protecting the countryside and green spaces from unsightly and polluting developments so that walkers can enjoy their tranquility and beauty
- Educating the public about their rights and responsibilities and the health and environmental benefits of walking so that everyone can enjoy our wonderful heritage

www.ramblers.org.uk

CROSSING THE FROG AND TOAD

Which comes first, wildlife or the car? All too often it's the latter, but in 2005 Powys county council launched a new experiment that reversed the trend, and the results were very promising. The trial came about in spring, when toads, frogs and newts begin their annual migration back to lakes all over the country where they spawned to start the breeding process all over again. The trouble is, their migratory routes often involve crossing roads, and in Powys, the area around Llan-drindod Wells had seen a plummet from 10,000 to 3,000 toads alone, partly thanks to their destruction by traffic. So the council took a major step: they closed the main lakeside road for 10 days. Not only did this protect the toads, it also protected the volunteers who spent their evenings helping the amphibians struggle over the steep kerbs on their way back to the lake.

Nice to see the car taking second place for once.

COUNTRY CONTEMPLATIONS

It was a perfect day
For sowing; just
As sweet and dry was the ground
As tobacco-dust.

I tasted deep the hour
Between the far
Owl's chuckling first soft cry
And the first star.

A long stretched hour it was;
Nothing undone
Remained; the early seeds
All safely sown.

And now, hark at the rain,
Windless and light,
Half a kiss, half a tear,
Saying good-night.

Edward Thomas, *Sowing*

GOT A PAIN IN ME VELVET SHANK

British fungi that sound like particularly painful afflictions:

Verdigris navel • Drab tooth
White spindles
Jelly ear • Choke
Devil's fingers
Aspen tongue • Leafy brain
Yellow stainer • Cramp balls

BATTLE FOR THE NORTH

There are two reasons for visiting Conundrum farm, the most northerly farm in England. The first is that... well, it's the most northerly farm in England, and some people like to tick these sorts of things off. The second is that it's at Halidon Hill, the site of the mighty battle in 1333 between the Scots and English to determine ownership of Berwick-upon-Tweed, the, er, most northerly town in England. There's a trail from the farm around the Hill, from which you can see the exact spots where the battle took place, and enjoy a good countryside stroll into the Scottish borders. If that all seems too strenuous, there's fly-fishing on offer, too.

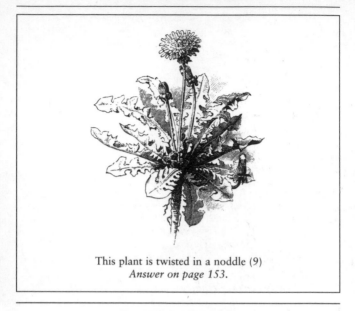

This plant is twisted in a noddle (9)
Answer on page 153.

QUOTE UNQUOTE

The outside of a horse is good for the inside of a man.
Winston Churchill, British Prime Minister

THREE INTO ONE

What do you call the combined forces of English Nature, the Countryside Agency and the Rural Development Service? The answer is Natural England, the name given to the new government agency announced in March 2005 that will aim both to conserve England's wildlife and landscape, and to encourage the public to get out there and enjoy it. But of course, three into one doesn't really fit, and approximately 600 jobs were expected to go between the announcement and the actual setting up of the new body in 2007. At the point that this book went to print, estimates stood at £40 million for the creation of this new agency, money expected to be recouped by about 2010.

Will Natural England achieve what Sir Martin Doughty, chair of English Nature, described as 'one strong voice speaking out for the needs of rural, urban, maritime and coastal areas'? Watch those green spaces to find out.

ECHOES OF THE PAST

Echo Lodge Meadow, near Wootton Bassett, is now one of the Wiltshire Wildlife Trust's most delightful nature reserves. Like many of today's reserves, it was once part of working land. The following account is of the young life of Elizabeth 'Doll' Davis, a girl who a century ago lived at Echo Lodge, and rolled up her sleeves to pitch in with the farm work along with the rest of her family.

In October 1908 we went to live at Echo Lodge, Wood Lane, Brinkworth. It was a small farm of about 40 acres. Very poor ground.

In our early days, my brother Joe and I played in Webbs Wood which surrounded our farm. We collected enough tree roots to make good fires during the winter, and dry leaves to litter the pigs, and the cows (of which we kept about 10).

Dad enjoyed a day's hunting on a 'retired' horse given to him by Col. Wm Fuller, the master of Crickland VWH foxhounds, who had the hunting rights of Webbs Wood, which belonged then to Mr Longley, a very nice gentleman who lived at Haywards Heath, Sussex. He sold the shooting rights to a farmer and several business men: Mr Geo Twine of Hunts Mill, Wootton Bassett; Mr Henry Weston, a grocer in WB; Mr Wright, a corn merchant also of WB; and Mr Brown of Purton, an independent man. Dad reared young pheasants for them, and naturally there were always plenty of rabbits, pigeons and an occasional woodcock for them to shoot. On shooting days we stayed indoors. Mother prepared a sitting room for the 'guns' to have

lunch. They always left us rabbits and cash.

We had a good orchard, and in October and November we picked the apples and spread them in a spare bedroom on straw. I enjoyed climbing the trees.

In Webbs Wood there were nuts galore, also blackberries. We packed nuts into stone jars, covered them with thick brown paper and buried the jars in the garden, to preserve the nuts until Christmas. We picked blackberries and sold them to the man who bought our surplus eggs. Mother also made a good store of blackberry and apple jam.

Dad rented a plot of arable land from Mr Lemuel Iles, (100 acre farm) nearby, and when I was about 16, I helped Dad by hoeing mangolds, planting potatoes and stooking sheaves of wheat. Not wearing watches, we stuck a stick in the ground. When the sun reached the stick, we knew it was dinner time.

In the winter, I did chaff-cutting, mangold-cutting, and helped Dad mix it and put it into baskets to feed the cows. Wheat was threshed and stored in a loft. Mr Hitchcock's man (Jim Ody) who delivered the pigs' meal, would take a sack of wheat to Brinkworth Mill when required and have it stone ground into flour.

We had a large oven which I heated until it was white hot, using faggots of wood. I scraped out the wood ash and mopped the oven clean. In the meantime mother was preparing bread and lard cakes. I filled the oven, using a peel on a long handle. When the loaves were baked and turned out to cool on a scrubbed table, you can imagine how much we looked forward to the next meal.

Cheese was delivered to us weekly from a neighbouring farm for sixpence per lb. Occasionally if we needed more, I went to the farm for it, Penns Lodge, Brinkworth. To see large vats full of milk, and cheeses in different stages of maturity in a large cool dairy, was a sight which thrilled me. My Dad would not allow me to learn to milk a cow, though brother Perce was expected to do so

before walking 2½ miles to school.

I carried the warm milk to the separator and separated it. We made butter once a week and took it to Hook Post Office and General Stores. In the summer when milk was plentiful we were paid nine pence per lb for it. Mother put some into earthenware jars with extra salt to preserve it until the winter when butter was scarce and we were then paid one shilling and twopence, or one shilling and threepence per lb, so we used our store. Sometimes when the weather was hot we had difficulty in dividing the buttermilk from the butter. We then slung the churn into the well for the night and got up early to finish churning.

I was determined to milk a cow. In the winter while Dad had an afternoon nap, I worked on the Jersey cow and eventually succeeded in drawing – milk!

MEMORIES AND CONVERSATION

Reminiscences of country life, as recorded by George Sturt in the late nineteenth century from conversations with his gardener, whom he called Bettesworth:

Of the 'knocking about' that Bettesworth endured as a boy I should probably have heard nothing – for he would not think it worth mentioning – were it not that he detests the insubordination of modern boys. They are 'mouthy', he things; that is, they enjoy too great a liberty of speech; and they are pubhished too seldom. In fact, the presence of the policeman shields them, to their own detriment and to the annoyance of sedate villagers, from the chastisement they frequently deserve. Bettesworth's hands tingle to be at them; and meanwhile, 'Smart difference', he complains, 'when I was a boy. Law! I've been cut over with girt clods throwed at me as I bin walkin' across the fields, and laid there afraid to git up, let alone speakin'.

The Bettesworth Book, written 1896

ON THE FLY

Fly-tipping is on the increase along our country roads. The term is the name given to the illegal dumping of rubbish, and the cost is becoming horrendous. The following facts are from the Department for Environment and Rural Affairs (DEFRA) database Flycapture:

- The commonest fly-tip is a black bag of household rubbish at the side of a main road.
- Fly-tipping costs £100 a minute to clear up.
- Every day there are 40 incidents involving multiple lorry-loads being illegally dumped.
- Almost 28,000 fridges, freezers and washing machines were fly-tipped between July and December 2004.
- In the last six months of 2004 local authorities alone spent around £24 million clearing fly-tipping.

WITH AGE COMES WISDOM

2.00% of people aged between 15 and 24 are birdwatchers
3.78% of people aged between 25 and 34 are birdwatchers
5.81% of people aged between 35 and 44 are birdwatchers
8.13% of people aged between 45 and 54 are birdwatchers
10% of people aged between 55 and 64 are birdwatchers
6.88% of people aged 65 or older are birdwatchers

5% of all birdwatchers are aged between 15 and 24
10% of all birdwatchers are aged between 25 and 34
18% of all birdwatchers are aged between 35 and 44
21% of all birdwatchers are aged between 45 and 54
24% of all birdwatchers are aged between 55 and 64
22% of all birdwatchers are aged 65 or older

WHO'S BEEN SPIKING MY MILK?

Hedgehogs have often been identified as great milk drinkers (although it's not really very good for them), but one old folklore belief that persisted even into the twentieth century had them as pests... because they suckled the milk from cow's teats as the large beasts lay in the fields at night. As a result, they were often killed on sight by farmers, and up until the mid-eighteenth century, some villages even offered bounties for the corpses of the spiky little fellows.

Poor old hedgehogs, they really have had the rough end of the rumour stick. Before the milk scare (which began around the Tudor times), Pliny the Elder put it about that they were scrumpers – climbing trees and bringing apples down on their spikes!

COUNTRY CONTEMPLATIONS

Three days later, when we arrived in the Highlands, everything seemed too beautiful to be true. But that is an ungrateful thing to say: better to exclaim with Emily Dickinson, 'O matchless earth! we underrate the chance to dwell in thee!'

A matchless bit of earth it appeared that afternoon as we drove the five long miles from the station to our cottage. So quiet it all was, that a door might have been shut in the sky between the turmoil of London and the vaulted stillness of this great valley. In the limpid atmosphere every crumple on the flanks of the distant hills was visible, and the creaking axle of our old carriage made the only sound. As we came nearer to the mountains, a delicate shrillness crept into the puffs of scented wind. It revived the very soul, after weeks of the stifling atmosphere of town.

Mary and Jane Findlater,
Content with Flies, 1916

QUOTE UNQUOTE

*Let children walk with Nature, let them see the beautiful
blendings and communions of death and life, their joyous
inseparable unity, as taught in woods and meadows, plains
and mountains and streams of our blessed star, and they will
learn that death is stingless indeed, and as beautiful as life.*
John Muir, campaigner and nature writer

THE OTHER CONSTABLE

Most are aware of the works of John Constable, one of Britain's best loved landscape artists. Few, however, are as familiar with the work of his son, Lionel (1828-1887), whose short career as a painter – it lasted just eight years – was actually very successful. One of the reasons that Lionel is so little known is because he was effectively an imitator of his father: he taught himself art by studying John's work, and produced several very strong paintings of rural scenes, some of which even made it into the Royal Academy. So similar were they, in fact, that until recently some were thought to have been by John himself.

Lionel was altogether a more modest artist than his father. His works were rarely very large – 14 inches by 18 inches is his largest canvas – and his application of paint thinner and more tentative. He was fascinated by silhouettes, however, and many of his works contain trees, figures or livestock silhouetted on a distant hill. Of all his work, the idyllic riverside painting *On the Brent*, is perhaps his best known.

MILK'S OFF

**The fall in numbers of UK dairy producers
between March 2004 and March 2005:**

March 04	16,031
April 04	15,955
May 04	15,923
June 04	15,846
July 04	15,723
August 04	15,665
September 04	15,531
October 04	15,444
November 04	15,354
December 04	15,221
January 05	15,140
February 05	15,053
March 05	14,979

COUNTRY CONUNDRUMS

A cryptic clue:
Pedagogue loses head for the first MP,
formerly Minister for the Environment (7)
Answer on page 153.

A HELPING HAND

Champions of the countryside in their own words:

THE MAMMAL SOCIETY works to protect British mammals, halt
the decline of threatened species, and advise on all issues affecting
British mammals. We study mammals, identify the problems they face
and promote conservation and other policies based on sound science.
Specifically, The Mammal Society seeks to:

- Raise awareness of mammals, their ecology and their
  conservation needs
- Survey British mammals and their habitats to identify the
  threats they face
- Promote mammal studies in the UK and overseas
- Advocate conservation plans based on sound science
- Provide current information on mammals through our
  publications
- Involve people of all ages in our efforts to protect mammals
- Educate people about British mammals
- Monitor mammal population changes

www.abdn.ac.uk/mammal

LAST CHANCE TO SEE

There are a few species of goat with interesting histories that are now in danger of being lost through lack of interest and market, the Bagot being one of the best examples. Although some people believe it evolved from existing feral stock, many think that it was brought back to Britain by Richard the Lionheart after the crusades, and given to Lord Bagot of Staffordshire in thanks for his good deeds. It also bears a striking resemblance to the Schwartzhal of Switzerland, suggesting its import. Unfortunately, the breed has very few large-scale commercial applications. Although it provides well for a family or small community, its poor reproductive rate, with the resulting slow growth of the herd and reduced milking, make it of little interest to today's high-yield demands, and its population has slipped after all those centuries to just 200 breeding females. It makes a strking parkland breed, however, with its large curved horns and long black and white hair.

NO GROUSING AT THE POLE

It was a brisk spring morning, early last century, when Lord Lovat attended the annual conference of the British Ornithologists' Union at London's Restaurant Frascati, hoping to find an answer to a grave problem. He had been asked to chair the Board of Agriculture's investigation into the red grouse mystery that was threatening to ruin the rural economy. Grouse shooting was an important financial mainstay of the Edwardian countryside, but the birds weren't playing their part. They'd been dying for some years of an unidentified disease, long before the guns could get to them, and Lord Lovat still had no answers. Every landlord, sportsman and ghillie had his own opinion as to the cause, but none had been proved to be right. What Lovat needed was an enthusiastic field naturalist who could combine bacteriology with anatomical understanding, and had the patience to see through what could be a lengthy scientific investigation. Would he find such a man?

He did. One of the young speakers at the conference, still only in his early thirties and already an accomplished doctor and ornithologist, not only had all the required skills for the job, but the even temperament and quiet dedication of the professional scientist who will see his work through and produce thorough answers. Lovat hired him on the spot, and five years later, the disease was identified (it was caused by a minute threadworm that affected the birds' digestive process), and the grouse moors could return to normal.

Who was that young doctor? He was Edward Wilson, who in 1912 accompanied Captain Scott to the South Pole.

Frederick was just beginning to think that the ban on hunting with hounds might be a good idea.

THE HOBBY HOBBY

Characters you might meet if you spend a day with falconers:

Austringer	Trainer of hawks rather than falcons
Bowiser	Young raptor that can fly from bough to bough
Cadge-boy	The carrier of frames that hold raptors
Cast	Pair of hawks
Eyass	Young nestling not yet able to fly
Haggard	Bird taken from the wild in mature plumage
Jack	Male merlin
Jerkin	Male gyr falcon
Make-hawk	Experienced hawk used to encourage a younger bird
Mar-hawk	Hawk spoilt by clumsy handling
Musket	Male sparrowhawk
Red hawk	Peregrine in immature plumage
Robin	Male hobby
Tiercel	Male falcon

TEDDY AS HE GOES

US President Teddy Roosevelt was fond of presenting himself as a farmer, a hunter, a man of the great outdoors, just like so many of those who voted for him. In the run-up to the 1904 election, so the story goes, he spent one afternoon entertaining at his Long Island home a couple of delegations from the rural states. The first group arrived, and everything went very well – a few more votes in the bag. The second turned up, and Roosevelt greeted them. 'Good to see you, gentlemen,' he nodded, rolling up his sleeves, 'would you mind if we conduct this meeting down at the barn. I've a fair bit of work to do.'

Picking up his pitchfork on the way, Teddy led the group to his barn, threw open the door, and looked around for the hay. The barn floor was empty. 'John,' he called out to his son, 'where's all the hay?'

'Sorry sir,' came a voice from the loft, 'I ain't had time to toss it back again after you pitched it up when those Iowa folks were here'.

QUOTE UNQUOTE

Geographically, Ireland is a medium-sized rural island that is slowly but steadily being consumed by sheep.
Dave Barry, US humour columnist

AULD HUCKNALL – SIMPLY DEAD

There's only one thing you need to keep your village being so small that it becomes a hamlet, and that's a church. By that criterion, Auld Hucknall near Bolsover in Derbyshire is England's smallest village. It's got just four dwellings, in addition to the church.

But what a church it is. St John the Baptist has been modified by various generations over the centuries: its arches are Saxon, while the tower and north transept are Norman. The early English south transept was once early English, but was rebuilt in 1597. The Victorians then came along and restored the church by lowering the floor and rebuilding the east wall in 1887.

So why should such a church have been built in the first place if there was no-one living nearby? One theory is that the Black Death took its toll of the original village, effectively quarantining the land for some time afterwards. Eventually people began to move back in again, but Bess of Hardwick, who lived in Hardwick Hall a couple of miles or so down the road, cleared them all out in the late sixteenth century so that their dwellings wouldn't spoil her view.

Of course, virtually nowhere in England is truly isolated these days, even the smallest village. As you stand by the church, you can hear the traffic roaring past junction 29 of the M1 a mere two miles away.

COUNTRY CONTEMPLATIONS

Welcome sweet Aprill! thou gentle Midwife of May's Pride, and the Earth's green Livery. Methinks I heare the little sweet birds making ready their warbling Accents ready to entertaine the Rising Sun and welcome him from the Antipodes & those remoter Regions that have all this winter rob'd us of his comfortable beames & benigne influence. But now the Cuckoe is come and the laborious Bees look about for honey. The Nightingale begins to tune her melodious throat against May: and the Sunny showers perfume the Aire. The Dew hangs in Pearles upon the tops of the grasse; while the Turtles sit billing on the little gree boughs. The beasts of the Wood look out into the plaines: and the Fishes out of the deep run up into the shallow waters. The Fowls of the Aire begin to build their Nests and sencelesse Creatures gather life into their bodyes. The Sun with his refulgent rayes enlightens and warmes the Aire, and the little Flyes to Flock and swarme in it. Now the Muses try the Poetasters in the Pamflets. Time is now gracious in Nature, and Nature in time.

Matthew Stevenson,
The Twelve Moneths, **1661**

WHAT'S IN A NAME: G

Gatherer	Glass worker
Gatward	Goat keeper
Gaunter	Glove maker
Girdler	Maker of leather belts and girdles
Granger	Farmer
Grazier	Keeper of cattle in pasture
Gummer	Saw sharpener

THE COW JUMPS OVER THE TOWN

Is it the city? Is it the countryside? No, neither, it's art.

For a week during early 2005, commuters in Santiago, the capital of Chile, who were inclined to look up at the office blocks around them, might have noticed a cow standing in its own field on the flat surface of a 10-storey block in the centre of town. It had been kidnapped on its way to a slaughterhouse by a group of performance artists, and lifted by crane up onto the building, where it was milked daily.

The makeshift farm caused quite a stir, and as the artists pointed out: 'We wanted to question the limits of art creation.'

And the good news? The cow was eventually sent off to a nature reserve to live out the rest of its natural life – and not a hint of formaldehyde to be seen.

Bloodhounds

The bloodhound is the descendant of the oldest race of scent-hunting hounds. Part of the pedigree can be traced back to the seventh century, when a French hunter named Francois Hubert crossed two different hunting hounds to create a sniffer dog par excellence. Interestingly, in later life Hubert entered the monastery, where he bred his dogs more for the purpose of finding missing people.

The dogs were brought over to Britain by William the Conqueror, who used them for hunting deer (the name 'bloodhound' refers to the blue blood of the owners of the beasts over the following centuries, rather than the red stuff of the kill). The dogs started to be used to hunt poachers by the sixteenth century, and in 1805 came the first recorded use of them by the law.

QUOTE UNQUOTE

It is pure unadulterated country life. They get up early because they have so much to do and go to bed early because they have so little to think about.
Oscar Wilde, *The Picture of Dorian Gray*

WHEN YOU WISH UPON A WELL

Should you come across a wishing well, you'll need to do more than just chuck in a coin and hope for the best. Tradition states that you should stoop and drink from the palm of your hand three times, without speaking, while running the wish through your mind. You must never divulge your desire to anyone, or disaster is likely to strike. Singing your wish is most definitely a mistake (yes, Snow White, we're looking at you).

The disaster aspect comes about because most wishing wells are associated with a religious figure, most likely a saint, with whom you make a silent pact while drinking the water, a pact that you must not break. One example of such a well on the Isle of Man was written about by Juan Othigill in the *Manx Quarterly*, Issue nine in 1910: 'The celebrated well on Maughold Head is situated half-way down the face of the cliff sloping to the sea, and like most holy wells, is formed in shape like a horseshoe. Tradition has it that it represents the imprint of the hoof of St. Patrick's steed, when he took a flying leap across the Island — the healing and magic waters gushing forth as a 'testimony to the virtues of the message of good tidings that he carried with him.'

THE CUCKOO BUTTERFLIES

Various members of the blue butterfly family, especially the large blue which became extinct in Britain in 1979 but has since been successfully reintroduced, are well known for spending their larval, or caterpillar, stage of their lives deep in the nests of certain ant species. They're dragged into the nests by the ants themselves, and once there they spend the winter tucking into the tiny ant grubs. The question remains: why do the ants take them to their nests when they're only going to feed on their own offspring?

The answer lies in a sugary substance secreted by the caterpillars which is irresistable to the ants. The ants turn up to investigate, and the caterpillars hunch themselves up to mimic ant grubs. Believing that they've lost one of their flock, the ants pick them up and take them back to the nest where they deposit them obligingly in the brood chamber.

Incidentally, the study of these predatory species of blue butterflies is conducted in Europe by Maculinea Butterflies of the Habitats Directive and European Red List as Indicators and Tools for Habitat Conservation and Management. Fortunately, they're known as MacMan for short.

KNOW YOUR PLOUGHS

Cable plough	Steam-powered
Chisel plough	Tractor-powered
Disc plough	Tractor-powered
Ard plough	Comes without a mouldboard
Swing plough	Comes without wheels or foot (the skid at the head of the beam)
Single-furrow plough	Only one mouldboard
Multi-furrow plough	Two or more mouldboards
Subsoil plough	Used to break the soil
Riding plough	Comes with a seat

THE WEE BAIN

The shortest river in England is the River Bain, which runs from Lake Semerwater to the River Ure in Upper Wensleydale. It's a clear river that attracts dippers and wagtails, and can be crossed at the appropriately named Bainbridge, a village complete with green and stocks. The river tumbles over a picturesque waterfall near Bainbridge on its route, and passes near the ancient Roman fort of Virosidum. All in all, quite an eventful journey for a river that's barely 2.5 miles long!

A HELPING HAND

Champions of the countryside in their own words:

BUGLIFE – THE INVERTEBRATE CONSERVATION TRUST is the first organisation in Europe committed to the conservation of all invertebrates. Our aim is to prevent invertebrate extinctions and maintain sustainable populations of invertebrates in the UK, by:

- Undertaking and promoting crucial study and research
- Promoting sound management of land and water to maintain and enhance invertebrate biodiversity
- Supporting the conservation work of other entomological and conservation organisations
- Promoting education and publicising invertebrates and their conservation, and influencing invertebrate conservation in Europe and worldwide

www.buglife.org.uk

RULE OF THUMB

Your handy conversion guide for understanding agricultural areas, weights and distances:

Rod	5.5 yards
Furlong	220 yards
Imperial bushel	2,219.4 cubic inches
Peck	0.25 bushel
Dry quart	0.125 peck
Dry pint	0.5 dry quart
Ton	2,240 pounds
Tonne	2,204 pounds
Short ton	2,000 pounds
Hectare	2.47 acres

(Note that a hectare is 100 ares or 10,000 square metres.)

CHILDREN NOW LEAF NATURE OUT

A 2005 survey by the Woodland Trust showed that today's children aged seven to 14, increasingly divorced from nature, were largely unable to identify the leaves of trees. In the survey, holly came unsurprisingly top with 54% of the kids recognising the leaves, but the mighty oak, that symbol of old England, only came in at 20%. The horse chestnut was tucked in behind with 17%, but down at the bottom of the leaf list were field maple (9%) and birch and hazel (each just 4%).

Children, concluded some commentators, no longer know their ash from their elder.

VIN D'ANGLETERRE

English wine is a modern idea, right? Wrong. It's had a chequered history of peaks and troughs for centuries. The Romans almost certainly brought vines with them to Britain back in the day, but the plant may not have survived their departure. What is certain, though, is that by the time William the Conqueror was getting comfortable on the English throne, wine production was taking the country by storm, particularly in monastic circles. *The Domesday Book* records no fewer than 46 sites from Somerset to East Anglia at which wine was produced, and by the time Henry VIII arrived, he had 139 good-sized vineyards to choose from, 11 of which he owned himself (the rest being divided between nobility and the church). Henry's dissolution of the monasteries was a major reason for the drink's decline in subsequent centuries, however, and by the seventh and eighteenth centuries production had virtually ceased. The nineteenth century saw a revival, with at one site in South Wales an extraordinary 63,000 vines being cultivated. World War One removed many men from the land, and the vines followed, and by the second world war, commercial production had virtually completely ceased. The 1950s saw a revival which weathered the public confusion with the vastly inferior British wine (made from rejected EU grapes) of the 1970s and 1980s, to become the thriving and award-winning industry that it is today.

COBBETT'S CRABBY GOBBETS

William Cobbett, in his visits to the countryside in the early nineteenth century, was not always impressed with what he saw...

It seemed to me that one way, and that not, perhaps, the least striking, of exposing the folly, the stupidity, the inanity, the presumption, the insufferable emptiness and insolence and barbarity, of those numerous wretches who have now the audacity to propose to transport the people of England, upon the principle of the monster Malthus, who has furnished the unfeeling oligarchs and their toad-eaters with the pretence that man has a natural propensity to breed faster than food can be raised for the increase; it seemed to me that one way of exposing this mixture of madness and of blasphemy was to take a look, now that the harvest is in, at the produce, the mouths, the condition, and the changes that have taken place, in a spot like this [near Newbury], which God has favoured with every good that he has had to bestow upon man. From the top of the hill I was not a little surprised to see, in every part of the valley that my eye could reach, a due, a large, portion of fields of swedish turnips, all looking extremely well.

William Cobbett, *Rural Rides*, 28 August, 1826

QUOTE UNQUOTE

HERD OF SWALLOWS?
YES, OF COURSE I HAVE

Some avian collective nouns:

Crows	*Murder*
Dotterels	*Trip*
Eagles	*Convocation*
Falcons	*Cast*
Larks	*Flight or exaltation*
Magpies	*Mischief*
Merlins	*Leash*
Nightingales	*Watch*
Owls	*Parliament*
Swallows	*Flight or herd*
Thrushes	*Mutation*
Turtle doves	*Pitying*

COUNTRY CONTEMPLATIONS

It was near [a] copse that in early spring I stayed to gather some white sweet violets, for the true wild violet is very nearly white. I stood close to a hedger and ditcher, who, standing on a board, was cleaning out the mud that the water might run freely. He went on with his work, taking not the least notice of an idler, but intent upon his labour, as a good and true man should be. But when I spoke to him he answered me in clear, well chosen language, well pronounced, 'in good set terms'.

No slurring of consonants and broadening of vowels, no involved and backward construction depending on the listener's previous knowledge for comprehension, no half sentences indicating rather than explaining, but correct sentences. With his shoes almost covered by the muddy water, his hands black and grimy, his brown face splashed with mud, leaning on his shovel he stood and talked from the deep ditch, not much more than head and shoulders visible above it. It seemed a voice from the very earth, speaking of education, change, and possibilities.

Richard Jefferies,
Nature near London

COUNTRY CONUNDRUMS

Which is the odd one out?
Short prick, long cutting, bachelor, garganey, wibbut
Answer on page 153.

FUNNY FARM

A man is driving along a country road one morning when his car suddenly cuts out. He rolls to a stop alongside a field, gets out and starts to look under the bonnet. A cow is watching him over the hedge as he struggles to find out what's wrong, and after five minutes calls out, 'Reckon it's the spark plugs, mate'. The man is so startled, he backs away, then breaks into a nervous run down the lane, finally bumping into a farmer. He stammers out his amazing story to the farmer, who raises an eyebrow.

'Was it a large red cow with a white spot over the left eye?' he asks.

'Yes, yes it was.'

'Ah, that'll be Bessie. You don't want to listen to her, she knows nothing about cars.'

OTTERLY AMAZING FACTS

- Otters can swim at speeds up to seven miles per hour
- They can stay under water for up to four minutes
- They need to eat one kilogramme of food per day, 80% of which is fish
- Their territories are up to 40 kilometres, and they mark them with droppings known as spraints
- Otters can breed all year round
- If you're otter spotting, look for flattened paths through vegetation, and muddy slides down river banks

SPIDER-MAN OR FROGMAN?

The water spider is a fascinating beast. As do most spiders, it builds its retreat with its silken thread, but, unlike all other British spiders, it does so underwater. Once the web is spun into a bell shape between underwater plants, the spider moves back and forth to the surface, trapping air bubbles in the fine hairs on their bodies, and releasing them into the web. Eventually, they've completed their 'diving bell' and they can settle in to wait for their prey – nymphs, larvae and water mites – to swim past. Once the young are born in the air pocket, they make their way to empty freshwater snail shells, which they too fill with air until they're ready to graduate to their own bell-web production.

A(t)tractor.

COUNTRY CONTEMPLATIONS

The hottest season is after June – the season when, as I have said, the downs are to me most attractive. At this season my custom on going out on the hills is to carry a wetted pocket-handkerchief or piece of sponge in my hat: by renewing the moisture three or four times, or as often as water is found, I am able to keep my head perfectly cool during a ramble of ten or twelve hours on a cloudless day in July and August. Long ago, in South America, I discovered that the wet cloth was a great improvement on the cabbage-leaf, or thick fleshy leaf of some kind, which is universally used as a brain-protector. So long as the head is comfortable there is nothing to fear, the rest of the system being safeguarded by nature. Exercise keeps the body cool.

WH Hudson, *Nature in Downland*

A WALK IN THE SUN

23 July 1944: Peter Tait, a young lieutenant in the Royal Berkshire Regiment, describes a day in the countryside during the Italian campaign:

I was serving in Italy and that Sunday morning we had moved through a village called Levane and headed north to another village called San Giovanni Valdarno, which proved to be fairly empty. We had to keep looking in rooms and houses and through doors to make sure no booby-traps were about.

My platoon was separated from the rest of the company by the railway line, which was high up on an embankment, and we couldn't make contact with them at all, when suddenly the signaller got contact and we were told to get back over the railway line and join them. So we thought, right, it was a lovely sunny morning, as it always was, then, every day, and it was a Sunday morning.

A walk in the sun on a Sunday morning.

Anyway, we found a tunnel underneath the railway line, so we had to go through that, very carefully, because you could tell it had been mined.

Some of the earth was newly dug, so you had to thread your way through very carefully indeed. Got through to the other side, turned left, and at that moment, shelling began. Quite heavy shelling. So of course we lay flat on the ground, not in a ditch but just on a grass verge on the side of the road. The other side of the main road was the rest of the company.

It went on for quite a while, and then suddenly, my left leg moved up into the air a bit. Donk. Something hit my face too, and it eventually turned out to be a bit of an 88mm shell. So I was lying there and I said to the chap in front of me who was a signaller, I said: 'Have a look at my face, it looks as if it's been shot up badly'. And he didn't move and he didn't look round, and I said: 'Look, come on now, you've seen far worse sights than this'. Still he didn't move, and I heard later that he'd been killed outright. Presumably something through the spine, or through the head, I just don't know.

Well as soon as there was a slight slowing down of the shelling, stretcher-bearers came across the road, presumably picked him up, picked me up certainly, carried me back to a barn on the other side. A farm barn. And in there they checked my wounds in the left leg, face, bandaged up the face a bit and the left leg a bit, put a tourniquet on, and said to me: 'Oh, it's only a flesh wound, you're lucky, you'll be out for two or three weeks'.

So I was very lucky, I said 'jolly good', and they gave me a cigarette, and I just lay there, and the shelling started again.

They said no way would an ambulance come up until after dark or when the shelling stopped. So I just lay there, well, I don't know, what do you do, just lying there, and hoping the shelling would stay just on the other side of the road, and suddenly outside there was an engine noise, and one of the medical people came in, said: 'There's an ambulance turned up'.

So, Good Lord, I said.

So we, about two or three of us, I think, maybe six, not sure, can't remember those details, were bundled out into this ambulance. Got into it, and inside was a British corporal, and on the wall of the ambulance inside there was one of those things that used to be in limousines for holding flowers, a sort of shell-shaped long thing, and little flowers in it.

'Oh', I said to the corporal, 'this is very nice.'

'Oh yes', he said, 'the driver always likes to see flowers.'

'So, who is he then?'

'He's an American volunteer driver, who takes his ambulance anywhere, at any time.' This corporal had been with him through Africa, and up through Italy.

So off we went, slowly along, switching from side to side of the road, dodging the mines, and eventually got back to the casualty reception station. Don't know how long the journey was, not very long I expect, but, you know, just lying there. So I was taken out with a stretcher, and put onto a little trolley thing, and out came the driver. Middle-aged American, and I said: 'Well, thank you very much indeed'.

And he said: 'It's not you got to thank me, it's me got to thank you.'

So I said: 'Oh, well, thank you anyway.'

And I was wheeled away, and I never saw or heard of him again. And I think now all these 60 years later, that bloke, an American, just drove his ambulance voluntarily. He was apparently not a conscientious objector, but a non-combatant, a civilian, and he just drove this ambulance everywhere. I possibly owed my life to him, I don't know.

What happened afterwards, after I left? The company was almost wiped out at the next major line, called the Gothic Line, across Italy. I know no more about them. But there was that one man 60 years ago in the Italian countryside. That man, obviously, I will never forget.

QUOTE UNQUOTE

I roamed the countryside searching for answers to things I did not understand. Why thunder lasts longer than that which causes it, and why immediately on its creation the lightning becomes visible to the eye while thunder requires time to travel. How?
Leonardo da Vinci, for once in his life
struggling to understand a natural law

WORKING DOGS

Greyhounds

Greyhounds are a truly ancient breed: illustrations on Egyptian carvings suggest that they came originally from the Middle East, and they're even referred to by Solomon in the Old Testament.

In England, they were associated with the monarchy from Anglo-Saxon times, William the Conqueror's royal forests becoming their prime hunting grounds, and by the Tudor period, when hare coursing hit its peak of popularity, the greyhound was the dog of choice.

It possibly gets its name from the Saxon word 'grei', meaning beautiful.

OF RIFFS AND RICKS

Songs with an agricultural bent:

The Farm, Aerosmith
Chicken Farm, Dead Kennedys
Parchman Farm, Eric Clapton
Space Farm, Fu Manchu
Down on the Farm, Guns 'n' Roses
The Farm, Jefferson Airplane
Farm on the Freeway, Jethro Tull
Back to the Farm, Steve Harley
Things Ain't Working Out Down at the Farm, Thin Lizzy
And anything by The Farm

COUNTRY CONTEMPLATIONS

I chanced to rise very early one particular morning this summer, and took a walk into the country to divert myself among the fields and meadows, while the green was new, and the flowers in their bloom. As at this season of the year every lane is a beautiful walk, and every hedge full of nosegays, I lost myself, with a great deal of pleasure, among several thickets and bushes that were filled with a great variety of birds, and an agreeable confusion of notes, which formed the pleasantest scene in the world to one who had passed a whole winter in noise and smoke. The freshness of the dews that lay upon everything about me, with the cool breath of the morning, which inspired the birds with so many delightful instincts, created in me the same kind of animal pleasure, and made my heart overflow with such secret emotions of joy and satisfaction as are not to be described or accounted for.

Joseph Addison,
Essay (1672-1719)

HERE IS A BOX, A MUSICAL BOX...

A quick guide to the main characters in that most famous of villages, *Camberwick Green*.

Windy Miller	Miller, cider-maker, respecter of the old ways
Jonathan Bell	Farmer, owns fork-lift truck, hates the old ways
Mickey Murphy	Baker, rather stereotypical Irishman, family man
Mrs Honeyman	Chemist's wife, baby-carrier, relentless gossip
Dr Mopp	Doctor, nature photographer, leader figure
Peter Hazel	Postman, whistler, suspicious relationship with Mrs Dingle
Mrs Dingle	Postmistress, owner of puppy called Packet, never mentions Mr Dingle
Roger Varley	Sweep, village's good luck charm, owns motorcycle
PC McGarry	Policeman, number 452, bit of a pedant, also owns motorcycle
Mr Carraway	Fishmonger, fond of sailing ships, loves fishing.
Thomas Tripp	Milkman, owns a cat called Tabitha, drives slowly down country lanes
Captain Snort	Soldier man, lives in Pippin Fort, complete anachronism
Mr Crockett	Mechanic, owns garage, fills up your car with just two gallons
Mr Dagenham	Salesman, drives around in flashy car, sells helicopters

COBBETT'S CRABBY GOBBETS

William Cobbett, in his visits to the countryside in the early nineteenth century, was not always impressed with what he saw:

In all the really agricultural villages and parts of the kingdom, there is a shocking decay; a great dilapidation and constant pulling down or falling down of houses. The farm-houses are not so many as they were forty years ago by three-fourths. That is to say, the infernal system of Pitt and his followers has annihilated three parts out of four of the farm-houses. The labourers' houses disappear also. And all the useful people become less numerous. While these spewy sands and gravel near London are enclosed and built on, good lands in other parts are neglected. These enclosures and buildings are a waste; they are means misapplied; they are a proof of national decline and not of prosperity. To cultivate and ornament these villainous spots the produce and the population are drawn away from the good lands.

William Cobbett, *Rural Rides*, 31 October, 1822

A HELPING HAND

Champions of the countryside in their own words:

THE BRITISH MYCOLOGICAL SOCIETY (BMS) was founded in 1896 and has some 2000 members from many countries around the world, reflecting its international status. Its sole objective is to promote mycology in all its aspects. This is achieved by:

- Meetings and symposia with international programmes, including a Young Mycologists' Meeting; and the Berkeley Award Lecture which is given by a professional member of 35 years or younger.
- Journals and other publications.
- Forays and workshops for field mycologists.

The Society is also active in the promotion of conservation and field mycology and in education through schools, universities and with the general public.

Membership is open to anyone with an interest in any aspect of mycology. Anyone uncertain of their depth of interest in mycology may prefer to join the Society as an Associate or join one of the regional fungus recording groups.

www.britmycolsoc.org.uk

SADDLE UP

So you thought that hammers and knives were all you needed to become a saddler? Think again. To make the perfect nineteenth century saddle, and harness to boot, you'll need to invest in the following tools, and then you'll be sitting pretty:

Pricking iron • Wheel pricker
Screw race • Double crease
Single crease • Compasses
Punch • Edge trimmer • Spokeshave

NOW THAT'S A GRID IDEA

Cattle grids: they keep livestock where you want them, and rattle the teeth if you drive too quickly over them. Unfortunately, they can also represent death traps for small mammals that fall into them.

Not necessarily. A Scottish husband and wife team in 2003 launched a new range of environment-friendly grids, which come complete with little ladders underneath the upper section, allowing creatures that fall in to crawl back out again.

As long as they don't do so when a car is passing over...

Mow around all this flower (6)
Answer on page 153.

THE LUCKTHORN?

The blackthorn has had a chequered background when it comes to superstitions, variously seen as a holy tree in medieval times, and as a symbol of evil. It was the pure white blossom that appeared on leafless branches that gave it its heavenly connotations, while the darkness of its bark simultaneously suggested an association with more demonic ways. Some even believe that Christ's crown was fashioned from its twigs, and in some parts of England, it was fashioned into the shape of a crown, burnt, and then its ashes scattered across crop fields to encourage a good harvest.

It is also considered unlucky to bring blackthorn into the house – unless you lived in Hertfordshire, in which case a scorched crown of the plant, hung up on New Year's morning, brought good luck.

All in all, it's a plant as convoluted in folklore as its twisted branches make it in the hedgerows.

THE POOR CLARE

John Clare (1793-1864) was one of the greatest of countryside poets, his career launching to great public acclaim with *Poems Descriptive of Rural Life and Scenery*. Yet his work lost favour as the industrial age of the nineteenth century rolled on, and later critics found themselves preferring the often more heady works of the 'Romantics' – Keats, Shelley, Byron, Wordsworth and so on – by the twentieth century. It's only in recent years, since the environment has become an item on social and political agendas, that Clare has started making his way back onto reading lists again. It's been a tough passage.

As was his life. The son of near illiterate Northamptonshire parents, Clare rarely had much money to call his own, so little that he was often unable to buy paper upon which to write his poetry. He coped by making his own, from layers of birch bark, on which he sometimes wrote with an ink made of 'a mix of bruised nut galls, green copper, and stone blue soaked in a pint and a half of rain-water'.

On one occasion, having come into receipt of a poster for a local election, Clare wrote some poetry on the back of it. It didn't damage his voting prospects, however: he was too poor to have suffrage.

COUNTRY CONUNDRUMS

A cryptic clue:
When you lose the first layer (3)
Answer on page 153.

COUNTRY CONTEMPLATIONS

On occasions Whistler had been known to drift out into the open and become a sportsman. A man told me that he once persuaded him to go out with a gun, and he told me he had not been out long before the most extraordinary thing happened. 'Suddenly,' he said, 'Whistler had a marvellous chance. A large bird – it might have been a peacock – came sailing majestically up to him. I whispered to him, "Now's your chance!" Whistler, having been brought up at West Point, knew all about loading. He soon loaded his gun, fixed his eyeglass, and fired; and – it was a most extraordinary coincidence, but – the next thing I realised was that my favourite dog was shot. Nothing more was said, and somehow or other we drifted back home. That was the only day's sport I ever had with Whistler.' When I told the Master this story, he laughed, and said: 'Yes: I did shoot the dog. It was a dog without artistic habits, and had placed itself badly in relation to the landscape.'

Mortimer Menpes, *Whistler as I knew him*
from his biography of American artist James McNeill Whistler

MEMORIES AND CONVERSATION

Reminiscences of southern counties country life, as recorded by George Sturt in the late nineteenth century from conversations with his gardener, whom he called Bettesworth:

'I remembers one time when I was helpin' Beagley at a job over there at ol' Miss Lawrence's at Cashford. There was air-brickes, you know, right along by the ground for ventilatin' the floors. The bees had found this out, an' made a nest right in under her parlour floor, an' they used to come up through somewhere... Well, I laughed an' I gits a long stick an' I pokes it into one o' these here holes. Out they all come – oh, ther' must ha' bin thousands and thousands of 'em – and then I did laugh. We all got out o' the way 's fast as we could. Miss Lawrence run, and the servant she run, an' so did the man what was there. He was lame, an' he went hoppin' off!...

'I was had in five or six places: but Beagley he on'y laughed an' said, "That jest serves you right for makin' a game of 'em. They never touched he. And he went indoors an' fetched up the floor, an' chucked all the stuff out – sand and bees and all – with his hands. There is some like that, as bees won't touch; and others, ye see, they don't dare go near where they be.'

The Bettesworth Book, written 1896

QUOTE UNQUOTE

I have never understood why anybody agreed to go on being a rustic after about 1400.
Kingsley Amis, *The Green Man*

A SHIRE THING

Shire Books is one of the oldest remaining independent publishers of titles about the countryside (and other subjects). Founded in 1962, the company has published over 500 titles, ranging from *Almshouses* to *The Barnacle Goose, Capability Brown* to *Duck Decoys, The English Rose Garden* to *Old Fishing Tackle*. As they very succinctly point out, their objective is: 'to publish authoritative, well-written and well-illustrated books, by experts on the subject, and to keep the price low in order to encourage the purchaser to satisfy his or her curiosity.'

You can find their books in museum shops, cathedrals, churches, antique shops, heritage centres, and of course some bookshops. If you haven't come across these great little books, satisfy your own curiosity by visiting their website at www.shirebooks.co.uk.

THEY'RE WELCOME IN THE HILLSIDES

In 2002, Plantlife International ran a survey to find the preferred county wild flowers of the UK. The results in from the Welsh jury were:

Anglesey	*Spotted rock-rose*
Brecknockshire	*Cuckooflower*
Caernarvonshire	*Snowdon lily*
Cardiff	*Wild leek*
Cardiganshire	*Bog-rosemary*
Carmarthenshire	*Whorled caraway*
Denbighshire	*Limestone woundwort*
Flintshire	*Bell heather*
Glamorgan	*Yellow whitlow grass*
Merioneth	*Welsh poppy*
Monmouthshire	*Foxglove*
Montgomeryshire	*Spiked speedwell*
Pembrokeshire	*Thrift*
Radnorshire	*Radnor lily*

WI OH WI OH WI?

Village branches of the Women's Institute; a parish newsletter; the remote areas of western Cornwall: all the ingredients for a gentle rural existence, you might think. Not a bit of it. In 2005, the editor of *The Chronicle*, which serves a dozen villages in the south-westerly tip of Britain, took a few liberties in his publication, with the Women's Institute... and immediately found himself out of a job.

The offending issue was a special edition, a tribute to the local history and efforts of the WI, that the editor decided to spice up a little with a few gags.

The alarm bells started ringing straightaway among the readers, when they discovered that their news page had been renamed 'News from the WI fronts'. Then they noticed that an advice column was now being written by an 'agony uncle', who discussed whether local women faked their sneezes. A new column written by a reader's dog just made things worse, as did a spoof article about an annual village witch-hunt.

The 'cut-out-and-keep' celebratory 'WI fronts', however, were the final straw. Subscription to the newsletter halved overnight, with threats of many more desertions to come. One village cancelled en masse.

'I was just trying to spice it up a bit', said the rapidly sacked editor.

Still, it wasn't all bad. He may not be able to join the WI himself, but at least he proved he was capable of making his own jam.

High level
(Cloud base above 6,000m)

Cirrus: Wispy, high, white distant looking patches, stretching across the sky. Often described as looking like mares' tails.

Cirrocumulus: Sheets of organised bands of high clouds having a grainy or tufted appearance.

Cirrostratus: Extensive sheets of transparent whitish cloud either fibrous or smooth textured which sometimes produce halos around the sun.

Medium level
(Cloud base 2-6,000m)

Altocumulus: Patterned, white or greyish cloud deck consisting of mainly rounded elements. Frequently in layers, with a roll or honeycomb appearance. Occurs in patches or long bands and sometimes covers the entire sky.

Altostratus: Greyish or bluish uniform sheet of cloud with very little texture. Usually thicker, greyer and lower in altitude than cirrostratus. Does not exhibit halos.

Stratocumulus: Low, distinct, grey or whitish cloud elements with a well defined rounded appearance often merged or organised into rolls or streets. The flat even bases have darker patches.

Low level
(Cloud base below 2,000m)

Nimbostratus: Layered rain cloud. Dark grey clouds with little visible structure. Usually covers the entire sky and completely hides the sun. Continuous rain is produced in the summer and snow in the winter.

Stratus: Low, uniform, featureless layer of cloud found above a land or water surface. Sometimes produces light drizzle. Known as hill fog when on high ground.

Cumulus: Fair weather clouds with well defined bases, little vertical extent, producing no precipitation and rarely covering more than half the sky.

Up to 12,000m and vertical

Cumulonimbus: A towering storm cloud. Large (25 km or more), well organised cloud often exhibiting an anvil-shaped top. Produces heavy rain showers and lightning. Entire cloud can only be seen from a distance.

QUOTE UNQUOTE

For me, a landscape does not exist in its own right, since its appearance changes at every moment; but the surrounding atmosphere brings it to life – the light and the air which vary continually. For me, it is only the surrounding atmosphere which gives subjects their true value.
Claude Monet, French painter

COUNTRY CONUNDRUMS

What was the price of an oak tree in 1830?
a) 5d b) 5s c) £5 d) Five guineas
Answer on page 153.

FLORAL MCDONALD

The list of county wild flowers in Scotland, as voted for in a survey by Plantlife International:

Aberdeenshire	*Bearberry*
Angus/Forfarshire	*Alpine catchfly*
Argyll	*Foxglove*
Ayrshire	*Green-winged orchid*
Banffshire	*Dark-red hellebore*
Berwickshire	*Rock-rose*
Bute	*Thrift*
Caithness	*Scots primrose*
Clackmannanshire	*Opposite-leaved golden-saxifrage*
Cromarty	*Spring cinquefoil*
Dumfriesshire	*Harebell*
Dumbartonshire	*Lesser water-plantain*
East Lothian	*Viper's-bugloss*
Edinburgh	*Sticky catchfly*
Fife	*Coralroot orchid*
Glasgow	*Broom*
Inverness-shire	*Twinflower*
Kinross	*Holy-grass*
Kirkcudbright	*Bog-rosemary*
Lanarkshire	*Dune hellebore*
Midlothian	*Sticky catchfly*
Moray	*One-flowered wintergreen*
Nairn	*Chickweed wintergreen*
Orkney	*Alpine bearberry*
Peeblesshire	*Cloudberry*
Perthshire	*Alpine gentian*
Renfrewshire	*Bogbean*
Ross	*Bog asphodel*
Roxburghshire	*Maiden pink*
Selkirkshire	*Mountain pansy*
Shetland	*Shetland mouse-ear*
Stirlingshire	*Scottish dock*
Sutherland	*Grass-of-Parnassus*
West Lothian	*Common spotted-orchid*
Western Isles	*Hebridean spotted-orchid*
Wigtownshire	*Yellow iris*

LAST CHANCE TO SEE

The closest living pig breed to the wild boar of old England is struggling. The Tamworth, named after the Midlands town where it was first bred, descends from the forest pig which in turn was descended from the wild boar. An outdoorsy pig that's protected from the sun by its reddish colour, the Tamworth was much admired by Robert Peel, who gave it its Midlands boost in the early nineteenth century, and by the 1870s the breed was being exported in great numbers to the US. Today though, in Britain, it's down to a population of just 300 breeding females, even though it provides possibly the tastiest pork and bacon of all British breeds. If the name rings a bell, it's probably thanks to the 'Tamworth Two' – Butch and Sundance – who made a run for it while being unloaded from an abbatoir lorry in 1998 and managed to stay on the run in the Wiltshire countryside for a full week. Thanks to media coverage, their lives were spared when they were finally captured, and they're living out their days at the Rare Breed Centre in Kent.

FARMERS ON FILM

Behind the scenes at Hollywood have been the following household (or rather farmyard) names:

Bill Farmer, cinematographer, *Sasquatch: the Legend of Bigfoot*

David Farmer, sound department, *The Lord of the Rings*

Jon Childress Farmer, visual effects, *Monsters Inc*

Rex Farmer, art department, *Boxing Helena*

Tim Farmer, production designer, *Cribb*

Traver Farmer, miscellaneous crew, *The Punisher*

Zahrah Farmer, producer, *Teen Summit*

HOW TO BUILD A TAWNY OWL BOX

The best box is a chimney-style box made to mimic the hollow, rotten end of a broken branch, according to the RSPB. These may be surprisingly narrow and deep but the best box is of internal dimensions around 795 x 230 x 230 mm, open at the upper end.

The box can be fixed at an angle of 45° in a large tree fork, or slung beneath a sloping branch, or fixed by an angled strip of wood to a vertical trunk. Drill a dozen 5mm drainage holes in the bottom and spread wood chips or stone chippings inside.

When siting your box, make sure you don't place it in direct sunlight, as the heat can cause the chicks to suffer.

COUNTRY CONTEMPLATIONS

A pretty country saying tells us that Spring is here when you can place your foot on three daisies; and very certainly it has come, for the lawn is dappled white with them, and the water-wagtail spins over it on his slender twinkling legs; for he is one of the few small birds who run and do not hop. An unseen stirring is everywhere. There is a sense of personality in all that before has been so dead and still. There is something better in these early days of promise and elation of Nature's every mood, even than in those that are to follow when the full pageant of the year will have begun. For everything is new, wonderfully new. And the great clouds, like chariots, lowering grey and dazzling white by turns, race across the sky.

Pamela Tennant, *Village Notes*, 1900

IT COULD DRIVE YOU CUCKOO

Countryside cuckoo lore:

- If you hear a cuckoo before the swallows arrive, then sorrow is in store.
- When you do hear that cuckoo, take a look under your shoe. You will find a hair that will match the colour of your future spouse.
- Listen out for the number of consecutive cuckoos you hear, though. It will signify the number of years before you marry.
- Keep money in your pocket during spring: if it's there when you hear the first cuckoo, you'll be wealthy all year.
- Similarly, whatever you're doing when you hear that call, you'll be doing it all year. Be very careful!

THE TROUBLE WITH TRUFFLES

Truffles are associated largely with France and Italy, but they do grow wild in Britain, too... occasionally. A wet winter and a hot summer are the best conditions for black truffle growth, but even then you'll be lucky to find one (Lord Byron was fascinated by them, and kept one on his desk for inspiration). In 2004, however, one man and his dog were out for a walk in the countryside near Welwyn Garden City. The dog, Missy, began to busy herself under the earth, and came up with a largish object that her owner originally thought to be a stone. Having dusted the earth off, he realised it was a truffle. Sometimes these things are meant to happen: the owner was no less than Jean-Christophe Novelli, celebrity chef.

It being such a rare find, however, he could not bring himself to eat the truffle. Instead, it's on display at his restaurant, Auberge du Lac.

THE SAXONOMY OF A CHURCH

Tick off most of these, and you're probably standing in a Saxon church:

- The church has no tower or, if it does, it's central or to the west.
- Doors and windows are narrow with straight arches
- The church possesses a nave and chancel, and sometimes a sanctuary
- There are no buttresses
- Paired windows are separated by columns, and often placed high up on the walls
- Ornamental decorations contain interlaced lines, and perhaps leaves and scrolls
- There is no lychgate
- The columns are cylindrical
- There is no pulpit

MEMORIES AND CONVERSATION

Reminiscences of southern counties country life, as recorded by George Sturt in the late nineteenth century from conversations with his gardener, whom he called Bettesworth:

'One time, after I'd bin off for some years, none of 'em knowed where I was, an' they all thought as I was dead. 'Twas harvest time, an' I made my way down to Birdham, about seven mile t'other side o' Chichester – that's in Sussex, ye know. I got there one evenin' an' I went an' looked over a hedge – over a gate, I should say – an' there I see my ol' brother 'Arry at work 'long of another chap what I knowed from these parts. 'Arry didn't see me; but t'other chap, he looked up, an' he knowed me, an' he called out to my borther lower down in the field. "'Arry", he says, "who's this?" Then 'Arry he seed me, and he says, "Ullo! where d'you spring from?" he says.

'"Out o' the road," I says.

'"Where's your kit?" he says.

'"On my back," I says. An' that was true. I never carried nothin' 'bout with me 'xcep' 'twas p'r'aps a shirt or two an' a pair or two o' stocking's...

'"Well, d'ye want to work?"

'"Oh yes," I says; "I'll work."

'"Well, but 'ow b'ye goin' to work if you en't got ne'er a reapin' 'ook?"

'"Oh," I says; "I dessay some o' you chaps 'll find me one."

'"There ye are," he says; an' he flings down 'is for me, and I had to use 'n. He went on bindin' sheaves his-self'.

The Bettesworth Book, written 1896

A HELPING HAND

Champions of the countryside in their own words:

THE SOIL ASSOCIATION was founded in 1946 by a group of farmers, scientists and nutritionists who observed a direct connection between farming practice and plant, animal, human and environmental health. It is the membership charity at the heart of the UK organic movement, working to raise awareness about the positive health and environmental benefits of organic food and farming and supporting farmers in producing natural food consumers can trust.

Today the Soil Association is the UK's leading organic organisation, with over 140 staff based in our Bristol headquarters, in regional centres and working as certification inspectors across the country.

www.soilassociation.org

WHAT'S IN A NAME: L

Lardner	Keeper of the cupboard
Lighterman	Worker on flat-bottomed barges
Lister	Dyer
Litterman	Horse groom
Lorimer	Maker of horse gear
Lumper	Dock worker
Luthier	Maker of string instruments

WITH HIS BAND OF MEN

Little John, Friar Tuck, Alan-a-Dale, Will Scarlet – these are the men in Robin Hood's merry band that most know. But the outlaws that once hid in Sherwood Forest numbered many more than a mere handful, and possibly totalled up to 140 in all. Among the lesser known good-hearted criminals were Wat o' the Crabstaff, Gamble Gold the pedlar, Arthur a Bland the tanner (who was also Little John's cousin), Much the Miller's son, sometimes called Nick, and George a Greene the pinder, or dog-catcher.

There's also David of Doncaster (who sounds like a caller to a radio phone-in programme), and Gilbert with the White Hand, an archer nearly up to Robin's own standards. Will Stutely, though, is the most complicated. Some believe he's just another incarnation of Will Scarlet, others that he's an individual in his own right. Whichever it is, it is he who first brought Little John into the band, and a good thing too... without his giant friend by his side, Robin would barely have made it to the second ballad.

In the spring, at the end of the day, you should smell like dirt.
Margaret Atwood, novelist

COUNTRYSIDE SCENES

*The serpent seemed very nice and everything, but he
would keep insisting that, look, he was still convinced
he'd done the right thing in Iraq, actually.*

COUNTRY CONTEMPLATIONS

I have lately myself been moved to ask: why are the villages sleepy? Why are they stagnant, lifeless places of at most an antiquarian interest, where the picturesque tourist wanders about looking, often in vain, for the church-key? There can be no doubt of the answer. It is because the best young men all go away. There is no inducement for them to remain. The country-side is continually being drained of its best blood.

The reason villages are sleepy is because the farm labourers are wretchedly paid, miserably housed, and insufficiently fed. I confess to some impatience in reading in the daily press of a prize won by a farm labourer and his wife at the Lincoln Agricultural Show for bringing up a large family on low wages. People should not be encouraged to do this; they should be incited to demand higher wages. It was not stated what the prize was; possibly a sovereign. It was won by bringing up fifteen children on fifteen shillings a week ... If the day ever comes when these people, fed on gruel and bread with or without dripping, are called on to defend their hearths and homes – I ask our Imperialist friends to consider the point – they will probably put up a very poor fight.

RL Gales, *The Vanished Country Folk*, 1914

WATER, WATER ALL AROUND

We may think that concerns about local water issues are new – well, some of the specific problems are, but the principles are not. Back in the 1930s, W Ibbett, in his *Sketches of a Wiltshire Village*, recorded the events of a parish meeting that had been called to discuss a proposal from a government engineer. The idea was that they would gather up the water that emerged from the village springs, drive it through a process of dams and channels into a reservoir, then pipe it back to the village again. Constant access to water would be the villagers' reward, and it would only cost them a few thousand pounds for the privilege.

'At the conclusion of the meeting,' he wrote, 'after the chairman had noted our unanimous vote against unlimited water, a flood of oratory swept the assembly. Anybody having an opinion with the remotest reference to water aired it. My neighbour on my left said that he sunk a well thirty years ago for less than forty shillings. Thousands of pounds, indeed! My neighbour on my right held forth, like David, on the perversity of water springs. "In zummer-time", he said, "when anybody do want a woish 'most every day, water be scarce, and winter-time, when a veller don't want a woish no more'n once a week, there's water all over the pleace. Water," he concluded, "is all very well in its pleace, but I doan't hold wi' so much water."

There was the whole thing in a nutshell. We did not hold with so much water.'

GENERA KNOWLEDGE

It's a basic rule in biological nomenclature that no two genera can share the same name. So the genus *Turdus*, for example, to which the blackbird belongs, can be used as a name for no other animal that is not closely related to the blackbird.

But wait a minute! The dunnock, that unobtrusive little brown job that hops about in hedgerows, is known scientifically as *Prunella modularis*. *Prunella*? Isn't that the same genus as the plant selfheal, scientific name *Prunella vulgaris*? How can this be?

The answer lies in the kingdoms. Zoological and botanical nomenclature are independent of each other, so that a genus of animal can share its name with no other animal, and the same applies to plants, but an animal genus and a plant genus can share the same name. So, for example, some members of the white butterfly family enjoy the genus *Pieris*, as do some species of the plant family, andromeda.

Makes sense? Of course it does. You don't need to be a genus to get it.

QUOTE UNQUOTE

The country is lyric, the town dramatic.
When mingled, they make the most perfect musical drama.
Henry Wadsworth Longfellow, US poet

JEKYLL'S ART HIDES

Gertrude Jekyll, gardener extraordinaire and frequent traveller in search of new and exotic plants, was also – and not many people know this – a rather decent landscape painter. In the 1860s and 1970s, she travelled extensively through the Mediterranean and North Africa, stopping off in Italy, Greece, Turkey and more, and was often to be found with her sketchbook and paintbox. Few of the paintings were assumed to have survived.

Yet a collection recently showed up at the Surrey Local Studies Library in Guildford, and it contains literally dozens of examples of her artistic talent, ranging from, in the words of her nephew Francis Jekyll writing in 1932, 'Arab cemeteries, chalk-white against the vivid blue of sky or mountains, courtyards splashed with crimson sprays of Bougainvillea, ruins of Roman cities guarded by the sentinel spike of an Asphodel, the villa gardens with their riot of scarlet and orange, the changeless types of the Orient against a silhouette of flowering Aloe or Prickly Pear, the solemn outline of distant mountains against a sunset sky'.

BIRDING: THE RULES

In 2005, in response to the growing number of birdwatchers in the UK, the Royal Society for the Protection of Birds (RSPB), the British Trust for Ornithology, and several other birding organisations drew up a five-point code of conduct for birdwatching. The golden rules at the heart of the code are: Avoid disturbing birds and their habitats – the birds' interests should always come first; be an ambassador for birdwatching; know the law and the rules for visiting the countryside, and follow them; send your sightings to the *County Bird Recorder* and www/birdtrack.net; think about the interests of wildlife and local people before passing on news of a rare bird, especially during the breeding season.

ALL THIS FOR JUST 90 QUID?

When John Bull, a mason and the Elder of Pendeford, died in 1660 he left property to the value of £89/3s/8d. So what could that kind of sum get you back in the mid-seventeenth century? Here's the inventory (a stryke was a row, kine were cattle, twinters were two-year old heifers, and shuttes were sows):

Butter and cheese
Hemp and flax
7 strykes of rye growing
12 strykes of barley growing
7 strykes of peas growing
8 strykes of oats growing
8 strykes of oats and barley
2 oxen
5 kine
2 twinters, 8 yearlings and 4 weaning calves
A horse
35 old sheep and 24 lambs
2 hogs and 2 shuttes
2 old pairs of wheels, 2 old tumbrils and an old wain and yokes, chains, harrows etc.
Geese, ducks and hens

FUNNY FARM

Two cows are spending the afternoon chewing the cud as usual. Buttercup looks up and says to her fieldmate, 'Say, Daisy, have you heard about this mad cow disease that's going round?'

'I know', nods Daisy, 'terrible isn't it.'

'I'll say', says Buttercup. She ponders for a while, then adds, 'Thank goodness we're chickens'.

COUNTRY CONTEMPLATIONS

To look back over the familiar records which, in the form of a 'Naturalist's Calendar', are placed side by side in most editions of White's Selborne, is to understand a double pleasure. That best of diaries is one which is referred to, perhaps, more often at the end of the year, when one season's records and occurrences are being compared with another's, than at any other time. There is a quiet charm in turning the closely printed pages and scanning a chronicle which is all of open air and simple country detail. The very names of the common weeds and insects of the summer countryside take on added graces under the grey skies and behind the drawn curtains of December. 'Wild carrot flowers', you read, and you are back in the spacious sunshine of June; or a note on the burnet moth takes you among the flowers and grasses of hayfields still uncut.

But that is not the only charm of the calendar. There must have been a deep and tranquil pleasure for the two authors in the actual work of making and comparing the entries in the country diaries; in jotting down, year after year, the day when each first found the hazel in flower, or first heard the spring note of the chaffinch, or saw the first of the returning migrant birds. The two diaries must have suggested many like them to succeeding naturalists and observers of birds and flowers. But there should be room, perhaps, for an even completer record, which might well belong to every country house, and which in time to come would form the most valuable material for the county or local historian. Nobody but the historian who has been asked to write a record of the flora and fauna of a particular district knows how seldom such material can be found.

Eric Parker,
In Wind and Wild, 1909

DUM-DI-DUM-DI-DUM-DI-DUM, DUM-DI-DUM-DI-DOO-DAH

Question: What do the following four Yorkshire locations have in common?
- Knaresborough Status
- Ilkley Tarn
- Bolton Abbey
- Barwick Green

Answer: They're the four movements in Arthur Wood's suite *My Native Heath*. Still ringing no bells? Well, the last of the four movements, a maypole dance, has been the signature tune of BBC Radio's *The Archers* for over 50 years. So popular is it that Billy Connolly once suggested it as a national anthem for the UK!

HOW TO DATE A HEDGE

The best way, of course, is to look up the records. But if they're a struggle to find, or you simply fancy doing your own detective work, here's the simple '1, 2, 3' as pioneered by a Dr Max Hooper in 1971 (although be careful – some modern hedges have been deliberately planted with a variety of species, although these hedges will tend to have an ordered look, giving their modernity away):

1. Pick a length of the hedge about 30 metres long
2. Count the number of species of trees and woody shrubs you find in it
3. Multiply that number by 110, and add 30. The answer is the approximate age of the hedge

(Of course the simplest way to date a hedge is to compliment it and offer it chocolates. Hedges can't resist chocolates, particularly the soft centres.)

QUOTE UNQUOTE

Autumn is a second spring when every leaf is a flower.
Albert Camus, philosopher.

COBBETT'S CRABBY GOBBETS

William Cobbett, in his visits to the countryside in the early nineteenth century, was not always impressed with what he saw:

I slept at a dairy-farm house at Hannington, about eight miles from Swindon, and five on one side of my road. I passed through that villainous hole, Cricklade, about two hours ago; and, certainly, a more rascally looking place I never set my eyes on. I wished to avoid it, but could get along no other way... The labourers seems miserably poor. Their dwellings are little better than pig-beds, and their looks indicate that their food is not nearly equal to that of a pig. Their wretched hovels are stuck upon little bits of ground on the road side, where the space has been wider than the road demanded. In many places they have not two rods to a hovel, it seems as if they have been swept off the fields by a hurricane, and had dropped and found shelter under the banks on the roadside! Yesterday morning was a sharp frost; and this had set the poor creatures to digging up their little plots of potatoes. In my whole life I never saw human wretchedness equal to this: no, not even amongst the free negroes in America, who, on an average, do not work one day out of four. And this is 'prosperity,' is it? These, O Pitt! are the fruits of thy hellish system!

William Cobbett,
***Rural Rides,* 7 November, 1821**

A HELPING HAND

Champions of the countryside in their own words:

PLANTLIFE INTERNATIONAL is the UK's leading charity dedicated to the conservation of wild plants in their natural habitats.

Plantlife International acts directly to stop common wild plants becoming rare in the wild, to rescue wild plants on the brink of extinction, and to protect sites of exceptional botanical importance. The charity carries out practical conservation work, influences relevant policy and legislation, involves its members in many aspects of its work and collaborates widely to promote the cause of wild plant conservation. Plantlife International hosts the secretariat for Planta Europa, the network of organisations working for plant conservation across Europe.

For the conservation of plants in the wild to be successful, Plantlife International believes that it must become the responsibility, willingly accepted, of all sectors of society: businesses, institutions, landowners, farmers, individuals, and the wider community.

As Britain's leading membership charity dedicated exclusively to this work, everyone is encouraged to become a Plantlife member, and share the unique opportunity to become better informed about wild plants and actively involved in their conservation.

www.plantlife.org.uk

B IS FOR BUCKS AND...

Nineteenth-century Buckinghamshire terminology explained:

Babbings	Fagots used to heat ovens for bread-making
Bag	Cow's udder
Balk	A headland in a field
Banner	Stickleback
Barm	Yeast
Batchelor's buttons	White campion
Bennet	Grass stalk
Bissen	The milk of a cow immediately after calving
Bland	Light covering of snow
Bobbish	In good health
Bucks	Staging erected across a stream, on piles driven into the riverbed
Bull-hern	Male heron
Buzzard	Cockchafer

HOW MANY KINDS OF SWEET FLOWERS GROW IN AN ENGLISH COUNTRY GARDEN?

In case you were wondering, the list, according to
the traditional folk song *English Country Garden*, is most often:

Daffodils
Hearts ease
Phlox
Meadowsweet
Ladysmocks
Gentian
Lupin
Hollyhocks
Roses
Foxgloves
Snowdrops
Forget-me-nots

Although as by the time the song gets to the third verse about birds,
and includes bobolink, cardinal and tanager, one begins to
wonder just how 'English' this garden is...

COUNTRY CONUNDRUMS

A cryptic clue:
Oils around the fermenting tower (4)
Answer on page 153.

WORKING DOGS

Spaniels

Not actually game catchers, spaniels sweep the ground to flush pheasant and rabbit from their cover, leaving the killing work to their gun-toting owners. Cockers, springers and field are the main breeds of spaniel, and their energetic zigzagging runs across fields, known as quartering, and good nose for a scent, make them ideal for the job. They're generally bred to retrieve, too, and are particularly good at fetching waterfowl from water. Woodcock was one of the more popular game birds of the eighteenth century, leading to the naming of the cocker breed.

Spaniels have featured in English literature for many centuries, dating back as far as Chaucer, and although their name is an adaptation of 'espagnol', alluding to their Spanish origin, there are some who believe that their entry into Europe can be traced back to Roman times, thanks to trade routes with the far east, where the breed possibly originated.

Furlong.

REPTILIAN VERMILION?

Common lizards (also known as viviparous lizards as they give birth to live young), come, as a rule, in a rather nice palette of mottled browns, creams and black. But rules are made to be broken, and the little reptile has more colour variations than almost any other British animal. Yellow is a reasonable possibility, as is emerald green, while completely black lizards can sometimes be found, their bodies affected by what is known as melanism.

Melanism – an excess of the black pigment – is actually a fairly common trait in reptiles. Slow worms have been known to exhibit it, and there have even been records of people running in fear from what they thought was a small black mamba! Well, a melanistic adder can give you quite a start if you're not prepared for it.

Pliny the Elder, the Roman naturalist, was obsessed with his work. It is said he even had himself rubbed down after his baths so he could continue to concentrate on his research. Here, in an extract from his mighty tome Natural History, *he discusses methods of storing corn:*

Some persons recommend that granaries should be built for the purpose at considerable expense, the walls being made of brick, and not less than three feet thick; the corn, they say, should be let in from above, the air being carefully excluded, and no windows allowed. Others, again, say that the granary should have an aspect in no direction but the north-east or north, and that the walls should be built without lime, that substance being extremely injurious to corn; as to what we find recommended in reference to amurca of olives, we have already mentioned it on a former occasion. In some places they build their granaries of wood, and upon pillars, thinking it the best plan to leave access for the air on every side, and from below even.

Some persons think, how-ever, that the grain diminishes in bulk if laid on a floor above the level of the ground, and that it is liable to ferment beneath a roof of tiles. Many persons say, too, that the grain should never be stirred up to air it, as the weevil is never known to penetrate beyond four fingers in depth; consequently, beyond that depth there is no danger.

According to Columella, the west wind is beneficial to grain, a thing that surprises me, as that wind is generally a very parching one. Some persons recommend that, before housing the corn, a bramble-frog should be hung up by one of the hind legs at the threshold of the granary. To me it appears that the most important precaution of all is to house the grain at the proper time; for if it is unripe when cut, and not sufficiently firm, or if it is got in a heated state, it follows of necessity that noxious insects will breed in it.

There are several causes which contribute to the preservation of grain; the outer coats in some kinds are more numerous, as in millet, for instance; the juices are of an oleaginous nature, and so supply ample moisture, as in sesame, for example; while in other kinds, again, they are naturally bitter, as in the lupine and the chicheling vetch. It is in wheat more particularly that insects breed, as it is apt to heat from the density of its juices, and the grain is covered with a thick bran.

In barley the chaff is thinner, and the same is the case with all the leguminous seeds: it is for this reason that they do not ordinarily breed insects. The bean, however, is covered with a coat of a thicker substance: and hence it is that it ferments. Some persons sprinkle wheat, in order to make it keep the longer, with amurea of olives, a quadrantal to a thousand modii: others, again, with powdered Chalcidian or Carian chalk, or with wormwood. There is a certain earth found at Olynthus, and at Cerinthus, in Euboea, which prevents grain from spoiling. If garnered in the ear, grain is hardly ever found to suffer any injury.

The best plan, however, of preserving grain, is to lay it up in trenches, called 'siri', as they do in Cappadocia, Thracia, Spain, and at in Africa. Particular care is taken to dig these trenches in a dry soil, and a layer of chaff is then placed at the bottom the grain, too, is always stored in the ear. In this case, if no air is allowed to penetrate to the corn, we may rest assured that no noxious insects will ever breed in it. Varro says, that wheat, if thus stored, will keep as long as fifty years, and millet a hundred; and he assures us that beans and other leguminous grain, if put away in oil jars with a covering of ashes, will keep for a great length of time. He makes a statement, also, to the effect that some

beans were preserved in a cavern in Ambracia from the time of King Pyrrhus until the Piratical War of Pompeius Magnus, a period of about two hundred and twenty years.

The chick-pea is the only grain in which no insect will breed while in the granary. Some persons place upon the heaps of the leguminous grains pitchers full of vinegar and coated with pitch, a stratum of ashes being laid beneath; and they fancy that if this is done, no injury will happen. Some, again, store them in vessels which have held salted provisions, with a coating of plaster on the top, while other persons are in the habit of sprinkling lentils with vinegar scented with laser, and, when dry, giving them a covering of oil.

But the most effectual method of all is to get in everything that you would preserve from injury at the time of the moon's conjunction; and hence it is of the greatest importance to know, when getting in the harvest, whether it is for garnering or whether for immediate sale. If cut during the increase of the moon, grain will increase in size.

WHAT'S IN A NAME: T

Tapster	Barkeeper
Tenter	Dryer of cloths on a frame
Thacker	Thatcher
Tixtor	Weaver
Todhunter	Fox hunter
Topsman	Head cattle driver
Tozer	'Teaser' of cloth
Tranter	Peddler
Tucker	Cleaner of cloth goods

---

106 *Episode number of the* Tweenies *that contained the song 'Down in the Meadow'*

QUOTE UNQUOTE

DORSETTINGS

Thomas Hardy's Wessex was an intriguing etymological combination
of ancient kingdom and contemporary towns and villages. Basing several of his novels and tales in the region, his characters inhabited a
world that was recognisable as Dorset and surrounding counties, but
with the names changed to protect the innocent:

Budmouth Regis	is really	Weymouth
Casterbridge	is really	Dorchester
Havenpoole	is really	Poole
Melchester	is really	Salisbury
Sandbourne	is really	Bournemouth
Shottsford Forum	is really	Blandford Forum

COUNTRY CONUNDRUMS

Which law protects the following?
RUSTICATED CONY
Answer on page 153.

COUNTRY CONTEMPLATIONS

I do not know whether you ever heard of the patriotic movement our
grandfathers made in the matter of planting walnut trees. Most of the
large walnut trees about here are of the same size and age, and were
planted about the time of the battle of Waterloo. It appears that there
had been great destruction amongst those trees throughout the southern counties for the sake of their wood for gun-stocks, so our fathers
planted these trees to supply the deficiencies. I had this from a countryman who remembered his father telling him of it, a propos of a
tree, at Aston Tyrold, which is now just such a one as my large tree.
The walnut is not a very long-lived tree, judging from this; I should
say few live much over a hundred years. I know a row of these trees
near the Swan at Shillingford, which the last landlord there told me
he had himself planted, that are now forty or forty-five years old; they
are fine large trees, but not as large and grand as the Waterloo heroes
that abound in the Berkshire villages.

George D Leslie, *Letters to Marco,* **1893**

LESS IS MORE, MORRIS LESS

The Morris dance, like fox-hunting, is one of those rural pastimes that inevitably draws a response from people. You either loathe it or you warm to it: a neutral reaction is rare. Yet despite being such an iconic aspect of countryside life, the origins of the Morris dance are obscured in history. Theories include:

- It derived from pagan druidic fertility rituals
- It was brought back from Moorish lands by returning crusaders
- It was introduced from the Mediterranean some time in the fifteenth century, and was derived from the French Moresque or the Spanish Morisca dances

One thing is certain. It was first recorded in a will dated 1458, in which the deceased wished to bequeathe a 'silver cup sculpted with Morris Dance'.

SLEEPING ON THE WING

Butterflies that hibernate as adults in Britain:

Brimstone
Comma
Small tortoiseshell
Peacock
Red Admiral (in increasing numbers)
Painted Lady (occasionally)
Wendy Craig

COOPER POOPER

Lady Diana Cooper was, between the wars, the true socialite's socialite. Married to the politician Duff Cooper, she was the type of guest without whom your party would be deemed decidedly second rate. By the time of the second world war, she had become quite the icon in Britain, and was often to be seen on her small-holding near Bognor, pottering about the butter churns and generally 'digging for victory'.

A group of ARP workers were doing their bit for Britain too in the area, and spending their nights sleeping in one of the outbuildings. Or trying to. It seems that the goat that they were sharing their space with was a tad on the pongy side, and they wondered whether Lady Cooper might consider moving it elsewhere. 'How very odd,' Diana replied when the request was passed to her, 'just this very morning the goat said the same thing about them.'

LAST CHANCE TO SEE

The Irish Moiled, with only 230 breeding females left, is one of the UK's rarest breeds of cattle, and one of the main reasons for its decline is bureaucracy. By the early part of the twentieth century, the breed, with its wide range of colours including red, roan and black, was found across much of Ireland... but then the government got involved. The Agriculture Act of 1949 demanded that for an owner to register their bulls and gain protection from dilution of the stock, a record of the dams' milk yields needed to be produced. Few farmers kept such records, and within two decades the entire nation's pure pedigree stock had dwindled to just two herds. The Irish Moiled is a very good small farm breed, providing meat and milk even from poor grazing land. Today, the breed's society is working hard to maintain the cattle's existence. Incidentally, the word 'moiled' comes from the Irish word 'moal', meaning 'little round'. This describes the top of the head where the horns would normally grow, and is the equivalent of the English word 'polled'.

HOME, SWEET HOME

Not everything lives in a 'hole' or a 'nest':

Badger	*Sett*
Eagle	*Eyrie*
Fox	*Earth*
Hare	*Form* or *scrape*
Otter	*Holt*
Rabbit	*Burrow*
Seal	*Rookery*
Squirrel	*Drey*

PARSLEY, SAGE, ROSEMARY AND THYME

Why do those four herbs in particular appear in the old folk-song, popularised by Simon and Garfunkel, *Scarborough Fair*? They're there for symbolic reasons. Parsley is well known for improving bad digestion, and was said to take bitterness away, which in medieval times was taken in the spiritual sense, too. Sage is a symbol of strength, while rosemary represents faithfulness and love. Thyme, meanwhile, is a symbol of courage: medieval knights used to bear images of it in their shields.

The song is a plea to a lost lover to prove her love through a number of tasks and return to the singer. The herbs therefore symbolise the fact that his bitterness is gone, and he remains strong, courageous and faithful that she will return.

A HELPING HAND

Champions of the countryside in their own words:

THE NATIONAL TRUST was founded in 1895 by three Victorian philanthropists – Miss Octavia Hill, Sir Robert Hunter and Canon Hardwicke Rawnsley. Concerned about the impact of uncontrolled development and industrialisation, they set up the Trust to act as a guardian for the nation in the acquisition and protection of threatened coastline, countryside and buildings.

More than a century later, we now care for over 248,000 hectares (612,000 acres) of beautiful countryside in England, Wales and Northern Ireland, plus almost 600 miles of coastline and more than 200 buildings and gardens of outstanding interest and importance. Most of these properties are held in perpetuity and so their future protection is secure. The vast majority are open to visitors and we are constantly looking at ways in which we can improve public access and on-site facilities.

We are a registered charity and completely independent of Government, therefore relying heavily on the generosity of our subscribing members (now numbering over three million) and other supporters.

www.nationaltrust.org.uk

COUNTRY CONTEMPLATIONS

Hard riding and all sports which involve an element of danger are the best antidotes to that luxury and effeminacy which long periods of peace are apt to foster. What would become of the young men of the present day – those, I mean, who are in the habit of following the hounds – if hard riding were to become unfashionable? I cannot conceive anything more ridiculous than the sight of a couple of hundred well-mounted men riding day after day in a slow procession through gates, 'craning' at the smallest obstacles, or dismounting and 'leading over'. No; hard riding is the best antidote in the world for the luxurious tendency of these days. A hundred years ago, when the sport of fox-hunting was in its infancy and modern conditions of pace were unknown, there was less need for this kind of recreation. For there was real fighting enough to be done in olden times... Those who are fond of lamenting the modern spirit of the age, which prefers the forty minutes' burst over a severe country to a three hours' hunting run, are apt to lose sight of the fact that in these piping times of peace, without the risks of sport mankind is liable to degenerate towards effeminacy.

J Arthur Gibbs,
A Cotswold Village, 1898

MEMORIES AND CONVERSATION

Reminiscences of southern counties country life, as recorded by George Sturt in the late nineteenth century from conversations with his gardener, whom he called Bettesworth:

In the evening, when the day's hop-picking is done, comes the heaviest part of their work for Bettesworth and his fellow pole-pullers. Like a wise and careful farmer (Bettesworth admires the care which he suffers for) the master will have no horses trampling over his hop-ground. All the newly-picked hops, emptied out from the baskets into coarse open bags or 'sarpliers', must be carried out of the ground to the waiting waggon. Some fifteen or sixteen bushels these sarpliers hold; and now that the hops are so wet [the weather has been terrible] the load is a heavy one – a hundredweight and a half in every one, Bettesworth reckons roughly, adding that 'it takes two men to lift a bag up on to yer back'. And in this season, from the clammy load the water squeezes out and down the bearer's back 'a pailful at a time'. This across sticky clay, the feet slipping at every step. Finally there are the two miles to walk, and by the time that home is reached, it is dark again.

The Bettesworth Book,
written 1896

QUOTE UNQUOTE

It is my belief, Watson, founded upon my experience, that the lowest and vilest alleys of London do not present a more dreadful record of sin than does the smiling and beautiful countryside.
Sherlock Holmes, fictional detective

WEB SIGHTS

The silky threads of spiders are best known in the form of webs, but they're used for several other purposes, too. Several spiders construct retreats from their silk, in which they hide while waiting for their prey – the funnel spiders, often found in houses, are good examples. Many species use their silk to make egg sacs, too, which they tuck onto the underside of leaves, or in crannies in walls.

The threads are also a great way of getting around. When a male spider of some species mates with a female, he has to make sure he's not around afterwards to be turned into a tasty post-coital snack, so he uses his thread as an escape route. And those tiny money spiders you sometimes find on your clothing on warm late summer mornings? They've been floating around on their threads in the dawn breeze, dispersing themselves over distances of up to 100 miles!

No cesspit around this tree? (5, 4)
Answer on page 153.

SHIELD YOURSELF

Not for nothing are shieldbugs, those small greenish insects with wing-cases the shape of medieval shields, also known as stinkbugs. Cup one in your hands and give it a light tap, and it will stain your fingers with a bitter, oily almondish smell. It's a defence mechanism, of course, but it's not the only secretion that the insect can deliver. Its gut is filled with bacteria which it builds up from its plant-eating days. Once it lays its eggs, it smears them with the bacterial soup, which the nymphs imbibe once they hatch, presumably to help them metabolise vitamins as they grow. Shieldbug young are unusual in that they have no chrysalis stage, but several nymph stages, or instars, each stage developing a new aspect, largely of the wings.

CITIES CAN HAVE FLOWERS TOO, YOU KNOW

Plantlife International's 2002 poll of the country's favourite county plants was very egalitarian, giving the following English cities the chance to vote too:

Birmingham	*Foxglove*
Bristol	*Maltese-cross*
Leeds	*Bilberry*
Liverpool	*Sea-holly*
London	*Rosebay willowherb*
Manchester	*Common cotton-grass*
Newcastle-upon-Tyne	*Monkeyflower*
Nottingham	*Nottingham catchfly*
Sheffield	*Wood crane's-bill*

COUNTRY CONTEMPLATIONS

I shall never forget those early days in the fields; that was my first experience at real work. Old Launcelot had sent down to the school for boys and girls to help with the haymaking. I was one of those chosen to go forth and put my shoulder to the wheel, or my hand to the implement. About all I really did do, though, was to lead the horses, carry the wooden bottles of ale to and from the farm, or rake up the hay with the girls; but I felt very important, especially when the time came round to receive my wages for the task – a bright two-shilling piece every week-end. How strong the sun shone in the meadows! How strange and far-off the hills looked to be! And how beautiful the trees, and copses, and hedges were to my boyish eyes! I can still see the far-off corn-fields quivering with the heat, the near meadows trembling too, the tall elms like spectres, everything in nature stock still, as though it were painted so; not a breath of air, not a sound but the tinkle of the mowing machine half a mile away, the rattle of the waggons, the voices of the pitchers and loaders, and the young girls laughing and talking as they raked away behind...

How different it all was from the long dragging day, the smoke, and filth, and fume, the foul stench and suffocating dust and atmosphere of the factory! The sweat of the open fields is clean and sweet, yielded naturally; that of the other place, before the furnace, is wrung from your very heart and soul in anguish, leaving you faint, weary, powerless, and exhausted. The other is gentle, medicinal, corrective, and salutary.

Alfred Williams,
A Wiltshire Village, 1912

PUT A SMOCK IN IT

The smock is probably the countryside's best-known garment. It was worn by many who lived and worked in the country, particularly in the Midlands and the South, and enjoyed its heyday in the eighteenth and early nineteenth centuries. As the 1800s wore on, the smock began to go out of fashion, although one attempt to keep them going involved embroidering patterns on the breast.

Broadly speaking, there were three types of smock: the reversible, which lived up to its name and could be worn front to back; shirt smocks, with buttonable openings at the front, and coat smocks, which opened completely at the front.

Made from cotton or linen, in a twill weave, (known as drabbet), you could have any colour you wanted as long as it was creamy white (although a few examples in blues and browns were not unheard of). The stitching, or smocking, was usually uncoloured, and mainly featherstitched.

COUNTRY CONTEMPLATIONS

In the winter time the Rat slept a great deal, retiring early and rising late. During his short day he sometimes scribbled poetry or did other small domestic jobs about the house; and, of course, there were always animals dropping in for a chat, and consequently there was a good deal of story-telling and comparing notes on the past summer and all its doings.

Such a rich chapter it had been, when one came to look back on it all! With illustrations so numerous and so very highly coloured! The pageant of the river bank had marched steadily along, unfolding itself in scene-pictures that succeeded each other in stately procession. Purple loosestrife arrived early, shaking luxuriant tangled locks along the edge of the mirror whence its own face laughed back at it. Willow-herb, tender and wistful, like a pink sunset cloud, was not slow to follow. Comfrey, the purple hand-in-hand with the white, crept forth to take its place in the line; and at last one morning the diffident and delaying dog-rose stepped delicately on the stage, and one knew, as if string-music had announced it in stately chords that strayed into a gavotte, that June at last was here. One member of the company was still awaited; the shepherd-boy for the nymphs to woo, the knight for whom the ladies waited at the window, the prince that was to kiss the sleeping summer back to life and love. But when meadow-sweet, debonair and odorous in amber jerkin, moved graciously to his place in the group, then the play was ready to begin.

Kenneth Grahame,
The Wind in the Willows

WORKING HOLIDAY

For thousands of east Londoners in the early and middle twentieth century, holidays were something beyond the family means – with one exception. A trip to Kent or East Sussex offered good paid work, and the chance for a bit of a knees-up into the bargain. The work was hop-picking, and every year entire families would leave their homes in Bermondsey or Stepney for the east – children and grandparents too – and spend a week or three garnering the hops and helping the household budget. Accommodation was provided, as was entertainment, and the package would finish with a 'Hoppers' Ball'.

And yes, the beer was free-flowing, too.

THE COUNTRYSIDE XI

All of the following have been part of an England World Cup squad, (that's two ways to represent the country):

Gordon Banks
Wayne Bridge
Steve Bull
Ronald Flowers
Tim Flowers
Roger Hunt
Norman Hunter
Alvin Martin
Nobby Stiles
Tony Woodcock
Chris Woods

WORKING DOGS

Beagles
This is a dog that goes back a long way. Probably originating in the Mediterranean region as a breed, it may well have come over to Britain with the Romans, and was certainly established as a hunting breed by the time of the Crusades. It became a popular dog on country estates, because unlike the larger hounds it could be followed on foot as well as by horse.

Largely a hare hunter, as hares don't go to ground where beagles can't follow as rabbits do, it was used to sniff out the scent of a hare's scrape, and main habitat, where the hunter would simply wait until the hare returned. Today, the breed is sometimes used by police to sniff out arson accelerants at the sites of suspicious fires.

QUOTE UNQUOTE

I suppose the pleasure of country life lies really in the eternally renewed evidences of the determination to live.
Vita Sackville-West, writer

A GREAT NATURE WRITER

Richard Jefferies proves why to many he was the master of nature writing. After all, who else would describe the hazel nut as cunning?

So they went on and into the silence of the wood. The soft warmth brooded over it – the winds were still. High up in the beeches spots of red gold were widening slowly, and the acorns showed thickly on the oaks. Then past narrow 'drives', or tracks going through the woods, bounded on each side with endless walls of ash-poles with branches of pale green; carpeted with dark green grass and darker moss luxuriating in the dank shade, and roofed with spreading oakspray. These vistas seemed to lead into unknown depths of forest. They paused and looked down one, feeling an indefinite desire of exploration; and as they looked, in the silence a leaf fell, brown and tanned with a trembling rustle, and they saw its brown oval dot the rank green grass, upon whose blades it was upborne. On again, and out into a broad glade, where the rabbits had been at play, and raced to their hiding places. Here were clumps of beeches, brown with innumerable nuts; straight grown Spanish chestnuts, with spiny green balls of fruit; knotted oaks; and tall limes, already yellow and filled by the sunshine with a hazy shimmer of colour. Over the glade a dome of deep-blue sky, and warm loving sun, whose drowsy shadows lingered and moved slow.

After a while they reached the hazel-bushes, acres upon acres of them; tall straight rods, with tapering upturned branches, whose leaves fell in a shower when the stem was shaken. Nuts are the cunningest of fruit in their manner of growth; outwardly they show a few clusters fairly enough, especially bunches at an almost inaccessible height; when these are gathered, those who are not aware of the ways of the hazel naturally pass on, leaving at least twice as many unseen. The nuts grow under the bough in such a position that, in pulling it down to reach a visible bunch, the very motion of the bough as it bends hides the rest beneath it. These will stay till they drop from the hoods, till, turning to a dark and polished brown, they fall rattling from branch to branch to the earth. There again the dead brown leaves hide them by similarity of colour. So that, to thoroughly strip a hazel-bush requires a knowledge of the likely places and the keenest of eyes.

Richard Jefferies,
Greene Ferne Farm

*Edith had been delighted to accept the invitation to
her cousin's for a country lunch. A shame, then,
to be offered nothing but hedgehog roadkill.*

MIGHTY TRACTOR FACTORS

The largest agricultural tractor ever built is the Big Bud 747, made in
1977 by two brothers to handle their 8,000-acre Montana wheat
farm. Its stats make amazing reading: it is more than 20 feet wide, 28
feet long and 14 feet to the top of the cab. It weighs 130,000 pounds
with fuel in its 1,000-gallon tank and ballast in the specially made
eight-foot tall dual wheels. It pulls an 80-foot chisel plough and covers an acre per minute. This outrageous tractor was fitted with a 16-
cylinder Detroit Diesel engine retrofitted with the biggest fuel injec-
tors made and produces 900 horsepower.

And you thought the biggest tractor in the world was
a Massive Ferguson.

A HELPING HAND

Champions of the countryside in their own words:

THE YOUNG PEOPLE'S TRUST FOR THE ENVIRONMENT is a charity which aims to encourage young people's understanding of the environment and of the need for sustainability.

We want to give young people a real awareness of environmental problems, such as disappearing wildlife, the pollution of soil, air and water, the destruction of rainforests and wetlands, the spread of desert regions and the misuse of the oceans.

All our materials aim to provide balanced views to take into account the realities of the modern world. Sustainable development – industry with less impact – is the way forward.

www.yptenc.org.uk

OLD MACKLINGON HAD A DU'

How to have an agricultural chat with a rural Klingon:

du'	farm (noun)
wIj	farm (verb)
'ervum	horse
nIm	milk
qIm	egg
qurgh	bean(s)
yotlh	field (Not *surchem*: that means forcefield. A Klingon will laugh at you if you get this wrong. Then he will probably kill you.)

LONG GRAIN

Everyone knows the Anglesey town of Llanfairpwllgwyngyll-gogerychwyrndrobwllllantysili-ogogogoch (which means 'St Mary's church in the hollow of the white hazel near a rapid whirlpool and the church of St Tysilio of the red cave'), is the longest place name in Britain. But what's England's longest village name? The answer lies near Retford in Nottinghamshire: it's the village of North Leverton with Habblesthorpe. This mouthful isn't just a pretty long name, though, it's also home to North Leverton windmill, first built in 1813, and refitted in 1884 to give it extra height. A tar-coated brick mill, it contains in its gardens several examples of the millstones used over the years to regulate the size of meal required from the grinding.

Even the mill wasn't able to grind down the village's name, however.

There is a part of the wood where the bushes grow but thinly and the ash-stoles are scattered at some distance from each other. It is on a steep slope – almost cliff – where the white chalk comes to the surface. On the edge above rise tall beech trees with smooth round trunks, whose roots push and project through the wall of chalk, and bend downwards, sometimes dislodging lumps of rubble to roll headlong among the bushes below. A few small firs cling halfway up and a tangled, matted mass of briar and bramble climbs nearly to them, with many a stout thistle flourishing vigorously.

To get up this cliff is a work of some little difficulty: it is done by planting the foot in the ledges of rubble, or in the holes which the rabbits have made, holding tight to roots which curl and twist in fantastic shapes, or to the woodbine hanging in festoons from branch to branch.

Once at the summit under the beeches, and there a comfortable seat may be found up on the moss. The wood stretches away beneath for more than a mile in breadth, and beyond it winds the narrow mere glittering in the rays of the early spring sunshine. The bloom is on the blackthorn, but not yet on the may; the hedges are but just awakening from their long winter sleep, and the trees have hardly put forth a sign. But the rooks are busily engaged in the trees of the park, and away yonder at the distant colony in the elms of the meadows.

The wood is restless with life.

Richard Jefferies, *The Gamekeeper at Home*, 1878

MEMORIES AND CONVERSATION

Reminiscences of southern counties country life, as recorded by George Sturt in the late nineteenth century from conversations with his gardener, whom he called Bettesworth:

'That is a miserable thing, is toothache. You can't bide nowheres, an' you can't sleep, an' you can't eat... There, 'tis a miserable thing... I 'en't had it for years now, 'r else I 'ave had it terrible bad. I've put baccer in my teeth – I've even gone so fur's to put it in my ears.'

I shrugged my shoulders. 'I shouldn't like to do that!'

'No; you can't bear 't long. But I've done it. Roll it up tight an' soak it in rum an' poke it into yer ear the side where the ache is... 'T stops the pain for a bit, but it very soon makes yer head begin to jump. Tell ye what's another very good thing now, an' that's a 'orse-radish, tied tight round yer wrist. Ye see that's where the nerve goes to from yer wrist – up to yer teeth. But you can't stand it for very long. It doo give it to ye. I dunno but what the pain's as bad as the toothache.'

The Bettesworth Book, **written 1896**

QUOTE UNQUOTE

Observe always that everything is the result of change, and get used to thinking that there is nothing Nature loves so well as to change existing forms and make new ones of them.
Marcus Aurelius, emperor of Rome 121-180 AD.

DOWN ON THE AGRICOLA

Despite the huge variety of breeds, each of our main types of domesticated farm animals represents just a single species:

Cow	*Bos taurus*	Bred from the aurochs, extinct since the seventeenth century
Pig	*Sus scrofa*	Bred from the wild boar
Sheep	*Ovis aries*	Probably bred from the mouflon some 10,000 years ago
Goat	*Capra hircus*	Bred from the wild goat of Turkey, Iran, Syria and the Greek islands
Chicken	*Gallus gallus*	Bred from the red jungle fowl of Asia
Donkey	*Equus asinus*	Descended from the African wild ass
Horse	*Equus equus*	Spread around the world by man

COUNTRY CONUNDRUMS

What is significant about the following sentence?
'Matt, who's she?'
Answer on page 153.

WHY DO COCKERELS CROW IN THE MORNING? BECAUSE THEY CAN'T MOO

Cock-a-doodle-doo is the cockerel's way of announcing its territory, rather as the birds of the dawn chorus map out their presence every morning. Yet such a raucous rural sound has had bestowed upon it several other meanings with very human implications. Shakespeare, for example, had it in Hamlet that the bird crows from Christmas Eve to Christmas morning to keep evil spirits away, although it was believed in much of Europe that a cock that crowed at night could bring a death to the family. Crowing at dusk meant bad weather in the morning, while if you heard a rooster on your way to work, good luck will follow. In Scotland, meanwhile, the birds were once buried in church foundations to ward off the Devil.

YEW ARE HERE

The yew tree is well-known for its frequent appearances in church-yards. But why should this be so? There are several theories. Some believe that the shady, protective nature of the tree made it a good meeting spot away from the fury of the elements, and so a natural spot near where to build a church. Another theory is that the tree's deeply poisonous aspect was a symbol that warded off evil spirits. A third theory, which links in to the use of the wood in longbow-making, suggests that these valuable trees may have been grown within the walls of churchyards to protect them from livestock and deer.

Possibly the most uplifting suggestion, however, is that the yew, one of the longest living species and a member of a family that dates back hundreds of millions of years, was the archetype of the Tree of Life, a living symbol of longevity beyond anything else that man was aware of. The eternal nature of the tree, along with its protective reach, would have made it the perfect living, spiritual partner to the church itself.

COBBETT'S CRABBY GOBBETS

William Cobbett, in his visits to the countryside in the early nineteenth century, was not always impressed with what he saw...

Came through a place called 'a park' belonging to a Mr. Montague, who is now abroad; for the purpose, I suppose, of generously assisting to compensate the French people for what they lost by the entrance of the Holy Alliance armies into their country. Of all the ridiculous things I ever saw in my life this place is the most ridiculous. The house looks like a sort of church, in somewhat of a gothic style of building, with crosses on the tops of different parts of the pile. There is a sort of swamp, at the foot of a wood, at no great distance from the front of the house. This swamp has been dug out in the middle to show the water to the eye so that there is a sort of river, or chain of diminutive lakes, going down a little valley, about 500 yards long, the water proceeding from the soak of the higher ground on both sides. Here is a fountain , the basin of which is not four feet over, and the water spout not exceeding the pour from a tea-pot. Here is a bridge over a river of which a child four years old would clear the banks at a jump. In another part there was a lion's mouth spouting out water into the lake, which was so much like the vomiting of a dog, that I could almost have pitied the poor lion. In short, such fooleries I never before beheld.

William Cobbett, *Rural Rides*, 30 October, 1821

RAGGING ON RAGWORT

Unless you're a cinnabar moth, whose distinctive black and orange caterpillars love it, ragwort is not the most popular of plants. The reason is that it can cause liver damage to horses if it is mixed up in their feed by mistake. This rather unfortunate effect has helped give the plant a number of rather derogatory names in various parts of the country, including:

Ragweed • Cankerwort
Stinking nanny • Stinking Willie
Dog standard • Staggerwort
Mare's fart

HOW TO BE A VICTORIAN MILKMAID

- First of all you need to get up early. Around 5am should do it.
- Now you need your milking stool. It's likely to be that three-legged item in the corner, carved probably from elm wood and with legs of ash. It's got three legs so that you can lean into the cow without toppling over – and besides, three legs are better than four on uneven ground.
- Sit to the side of the cow near the tail with your face resting against her, and start to stroke two of the teats gently with a pulsing action that mimics the sucking of a calf. Then move to the second pair of teats and continue until your bucket is full, or the cow has yielded her full supply.
- Repeat at lunchtime. In all, you should get up to 15 litres per day.

A HELPING HAND

Champions of the countryside in their own words:

COMPASSION IN WORLD FARMING (CIWF) exists as a voice for farm animals across the globe.

CIWF seeks to achieve the global abolition of factory farming and the adoption of agricultural systems which meet the welfare needs of farm animals in the belief that this will also benefit humanity and the environment.

CIWF's aim is to achieve the ending of factory farming systems and all other practices, technologies and trades which impose suffering on farmed animals. CIWF works to achieve this aim by hard-hitting campaigning, public education and vigorous political lobbying.

www.ciwf.org.uk

MEMORIES AND CONVERSATION

Reminiscences of southern counties country life, as recorded by George Sturt in the late nineteenth century from conversations with his gardener, whom he called Bettesworth:

Said Bettesworth, 'There's a change o' some sort goin' on, sir. Down there at home, all the pigs be a'gallopin' round the sties and barkin' like dogs. I went an' looked at my two dinner-time. They was a-barkin' – a reg'lar bark it is, hwuh! hwuh! jest like a dog: an' then they went round after one another! I says, "Goo it agen lads! There en't no fear o' your gettin' the cramp all the time as you can gallop"'

Said I, 'I saw two little pigs in their sty up the lane here the other day, in and out and round about...'

'At play, sir?'

'Ah, like a pair o' kittens.'

'There ye are! There's a change a-goin' on. It's pretty near a sure sign o' bad weather when you sees the pigs gallopin' about in the sty.'

***The Bettesworth Book*, written 1896**

WHAT'S IN A NAME: M

Marshall	Horse keeper
Mather	Mower
Melder	Corn miller
Mercer	Cloth seller
Milliner	Hat seller
Molitor	Miller
Multurer	Miller

THE BATMEN'S BATSMAN

The Bat Conservation Trust (www.bats.org.uk) does exactly what it says on the tin – which is fortunate, really, seeing as every single one of Britain's bat species has struggled at one time or another in the last 50 years. The Trust monitors populations, advises on what to do if you find bats roosting in your home, directs research into the creatures, and co-ordinates bat conservation at local and national levels.

They've clearly got a sense of humour, too. Their patron – quoted as saying 'Bats are nothing to be wary of and certainly nothing to be frightened of. Indeed the more I learn about them, the more I realise they are wonderful animals, much maligned and often mistreated' – is none other than the cricketer David Gower.

Does this make him first in the batting order?

COUNTRY CONTEMPLATIONS

There is one small oil-painting known to me – it ought to be in the National Gallery – which I rate above all other pictures of trees that I have seen. This depicts only a lone-standing, wind-swept Hawthorn, a sturdy little tree, on the Sussex Downs. But viewing it you can hear the swish of the blast streaming through the low boughs and out-pennoning all the thin light upper branches that are struggling to escape its violence; you can hear the groaning of those warped lower limbs as they writhe and shudder in the wind's grip; and you can feel and visualise the agelong struggle that the solitary old tree has fought against its perpetual and implacable foe. There are few paintings of trees that can make even a tithe of that impression on the beholder! Yet there is nothing here exaggerated, nothing even slightly over-stressed. The grey of the east-wind-racked sky is there and the brown-green tones of the harried tree, merging into the brown-green of the downland bents among which it stands so firmly rooted. That is all – all except the imaginative power of the painter, which has compelled this old Hawthorn into line and colour, as the power of the magician in the Arabian Nights imprisoned the genii in a little jar.

Bertram Lloyd,
Winter Trees and Tones
(Sadly Lloyd does not mention the name of the artist.)

COUNTRY CONUNDRUMS

A cryptic clue:
I trust I can find inside something of the country (6)
Answer on page 153.

ITSY BITSY SUPERSTITIONS

Rural arachnid beliefs that will help you get through your days:

- If you see a spider spinning a web, you'll shortly be getting new clothes.
- If you walk into a web, you'll soon meet a new friend.
- 'If you wish to live and thrive, let the spider run alive'.
- If a money spider floats onto you, your finances will soon be on the up.
- Got a fever? Try swallowing a spider with some syrup.
- There's a trip ahead of you if you see a spider run down a web – only, though, if you see it in the afternoon.
- To combat plague, put a spider in a walnut shell and hang it around your neck.

ANIMAL MADJECTIVE

Want to sound truly knowledgeable on your walk through the country? Try pointing out the talpine mounds at your feet, or sniffing the musteline air, or listening to the ranine chorus. Here's a quick guide to some natural adjectives:

Badger	*musteline*
Earthworm	*lumbricine*
Flea	*pulicine*
Fox	*vulpine*
Frog	*ranine*
Mole	*talpine*
Mouse	*murine*
Otter	*lutrine*
Squirrel	*sciurine*
Wasp	*vespine*

QUOTE UNQUOTE

*The first farmer was the first man, and all historic nobility rests
on possession and use of land.*
Ralph Waldo Emerson, US poet and philosopher

TUPSY-DAISY

It's an old rural myth, but worth repeating, that there's an American countryside practice known as cow tupping, or tipping. This is nothing to do with the tupping of sheep, which is encouraging a ram to mate with a ewe, but simply running up to a cow and pushing it over.

One website, 'The wondrously random world', has even gone so far as to publish the rules:

'Welcome to the beginners guide to cow tupping. For those of you who don't know, cow tupping is a pastime widely practised in the countryside, and is currently pushing for recognition as a sport and entry into the Olympic Games by 2020. The basic rules are to complete the most difficult tupping, with as few attempts as possible. In competition, three fails at any one tup signals the end of a tuppers challenge. If two tuppers have completed a tup of the same level of difficulty in the same number of attempts, then a countback system is employed. The total number of attempts used in the whole competition is computed, with the tupper who has taken the least attempts to finish being the winner. If there is still a tie, then the speed of the final tup is used to determine the winner, and in the unlikely event no winner can be determined from this then the contest is declared a tie.'

Whatever you do, don't try this at home. Or, come to think of it, in a field.

WHOSE FARM IS IT ANYWAY?

It depends on which of these songs you're listening to:

Michelle's Farm, Beastie Boys
Maggie's Farm, Bob Dylan
When Alice Comes Back to the Farm, ELO
Miss Judy's Farm, Faces
Uncle Bernie's Farm, Frank Zappa
Animal Farm, The Kinks
Junior's Farm, Paul McCartney
Old Man on the Farm, Randy Newman
I Ain't Gonna Work on Maggie's Farm no More, The Waterboys

PLUS CA CHANGE

In 1903, H Rider Haggard, author of *King Solomon's Mines*, wrote the following letter to Asquith, then leader of the opposition and soon to become prime minister. Although some of the facts may have changed, the sentiments are hardly out of place over a century later:

My Dear Sir

I have read your speech reported yesterday, and in consequence I am venturing to ask your acceptance of the copy of my recently published work 'Rural England' which I send herewith. I hope that you may find time to glance at the book, and especially at the chapter headed 'Conclusions'. Most thoroughly do I agree with what you say as to the possibility of a vastly increased output of home-grown food. But this you will never get until you have co-operation and the cheap carriage which, as you may have seen, I am doing my best to advocate – under the form of an increase in postal facilities. For this reason: without co-opera-

tion and cheap carriage the small holder cannot thrive; and it is to him that you must look for an enlarged production – not to the large farmers.

As regards the lack of rural cottages I agree that this is one of the great causes of the exodus to the towns. But the lack of prospects is a greater. If labourers had a prospect of rising and could do well on the land as small holders they would soon get cottages, for then they could pay a rent at which these would be remunerative to build.

To my mind, to plunge everlastingly into foreign adventure after foreign adventure, however difficult and costly, and all the while to neglect our own land so cruelly is a madness. What will it benefit us to gain the whole earth if we are to lose our country-fed population? Again, with all this outcry about our danger from lack of food, why not take the obvious remedy of growing most of it at home, as we could do in my judgment, and without protection.

COUNTRY CONTEMPLATIONS

'Always get over a stile' is the one rule that should ever be borne in mind by those who wish to see the land as it really is – that is to say, never omit to explore a footpath, for neve was there a footpath yet which did not pass something of interest.

In the meadows, everything comes pressing lovingly up to the path. The small-leaved clover can scarce be driven back by frequent footsteps from endeavouring to cover the bare earth of the centre. Tall buttercups, round whose stalks the cattle have carefully grazed, stand in ranks; strong ox-eye daisies, with broad white disks and torn leaves, form with the grass the tricolour of the pasture – white, green, and gold.

When the path enters the mowing-grass, ripe for the scythe, the simplicity of these cardinal hues is lost in the multitude of shades and the addition of other colours. The surface of mowing-grass is indeed made up of so many tints that at the first glance it is confusing; and hence, perhaps, it is that hardly ever has an artist succeeded in getting the effect upon canvas. Of the million blades of grass no two are of the same shade.

Richard Jefferies, *Nature Near London*

QUOTE UNQUOTE

Of all occupations from which gain is secured, there is none better than agriculture, nothing more productive, nothing sweeter, nothing more worthy of a free man.
Cicero, Roman political commentator

LAST CHANCE TO SEE

The White Park is probably Britain's oldest native cattle breed. Remains of cattle very similar to White Park have been found in Wales, Scotland, Ireland and northern England from as far back as 500BC, and by the thirteenth century the breed was well established in several British park enclosures, some of which still survive today. In 1210 the wife of William de Breos (Brecon) tried unsuccessfully to appease King John with a gift of a bull and four hundred cows of White Park colour. By contrast, few cattle breeds can claim a lineage much further back than around 300 years. By the 1960s, however, only four herds remained, but thanks to the efforts of the breed's society, numbers have now climbed back a little to around 500 breeding females. With their bright white coats and lengthy horns, as they roam about in British parklands, they provide a stunning visual throwback to the earliest days of British bovine agriculture.

She used to be embarrassed by the unusual mutant growth sticking out of her back, but Josephine's friends barely noticed the giant slice of orange any more.

COBBETT'S CRABBY GOBBETS

William Cobbett, in his visits to the countryside in the early nineteenth century, was not always impressed with what he saw:

The turnips look pretty well all the way down the valley; but I see very few, except swedish turnips. The early common turnips very nearly all failed, I believe. But the stubbles are beautifully bright; and the rick-yards tell us that the crops are good, especially of wheat. This is not a country of pease and beans, nor of oats, except for home consumption. The crops are wheat, barley, wool and lambs, and these latter not to be sold to butchers, but to be sold, at the great fairs, to those who are going to keep them for some time, whether to breed from or finally to fat for the butcher. It is the pulse and the oats that appear to have failed most this year; and, therefore, this valley has not suffered. I do not perceive that they have many potatoes; but what they have of this base root seem to look well enough. It was one of the greatest villains upon earth (Sir Walter Raleigh) who (they say) first brought this root into England. He was hanged at last! What a pity, since he was to be hanged, the hanging did not take place before he became such a mischievous devil as he was in the latter two-thirds of his life!

William Cobbett, *Rural Rides,*
30 August 1826

Address, in Southwark Street, of the London office of the Campaign for the Protection of Rural England (CPRE)

SELBORNE DEFINED

Gilbert White, one of the greatest ever chroniclers of the countryside, describes his own corner as it was in the late eighteenth century:

The parish of Selborne lies in the extreme eastern corner of the county of Hampshire, bordering on the county of Sussex, and not far from the county of Surrey; is about fifty miles south-west of London, in latitude 51, and near midway between the towns of Alton and Petersfield. Being very large and extensive, it abuts on twelve parishes, two of which are in Sussex, viz., Trotton and Rogate. If you begin from the south and proceed westward, the adjacent parishes are Emshot, Newton Valence, Faringdon, Harteley Mauduit, Great Ward le ham, Kingsley, Hedleigh, Bramshot, Trotton, Rogate, Lysse, and Greatham.

The soils of this district are almost as various and diversified as the views and aspects. The high part to the south-west consists of a vast hill of chalk, rising three hundred feet above the village; and is divided into a sheep down, the high wood, and a long hanging wood called the Hanger. The covert of this eminence is altogether beech, the most lovely of all forest trees, whether we consider its smooth rind or bark, its glossy foliage, or graceful pendulous boughs. The down, or sheep-walk, is a pleasing park-like spot, of about one mile by half that space, jutting out on the verge of the hill-country, where it begins to break down into the plains, and commanding a very engaging view, being an assemblage of hill, dale, wood-lands, heath, and water.

The prospect is bounded to the south-east and east by the vast range of mountains called the Susses-downs, by Guild-down near Guildford, and by the Downs round Dorking, and Rye-gate in Surrey, to the north-east, which altogether, with the country beyond Alton and Farnham, form a noble and extensive outline. At the foot of this hill, one stage or step from the uplands, lies the village, which consists of one single straggling street, three-quarters of a mile in length, in a sheltered vale, and running parallel with the Hanger. The houses are divided from the hill by a vein of stiff clay (good wheat-land), yet stand on a rock of white stone, little in appearance removed from chalk; but seems so far from being calcareous, that it endures extreme heat. Yet that the freestone still preserves somewhat that is analogous to chalk, is plain from the beeches which descend as low as those rocks extend, and no farther, and thrive as well on them, where the ground is steep, as on the chalks.

The cart-way of the village divides, in a remarkable manner, two very incongruous soils. To the south-west is a rank-clay, that requires the labour of years to render it mellow; while the gardens to the north-east, and small enclosures behind, consist of a warm, forward, crumbling mould, called black malm, which seems highly saturated with vegetable and animal manure; and these may perhaps have been the original site of the town; while the wood and coverts might extend down to the opposite bank. At each end of the village, which runs from south-east to north-west, arises a small rivulet: that at the north-west end frequently fails; but the other is a fine perennial spring, little influenced by drought or wet seasons, called Well-head. This breaks out of some high grounds joining to Core Hill, a noble chalk promontory, remarkable for sending forth two streams into two different seas. The one to the south becomes a branch of the Arun, running to Arundel, and so falling into the British Channel: the other to the north. The Selborne stream makes one branch of the Wey; and meeting the Black-down stream at Hedleigh, and the Alton and Farnham stream at Tilford-bridge, swells into a considerable river, navigable at Godalming; from whence it passes to Guildford, and so into the Thames at Weybridge; and thus at the Nore into the German Ocean.

Our wells, at an average, run to about sixty-three feet, and when sunk to that depth seldom fail; but produce a fine limpid water, soft to the taste, and much commended by those who drink the pure element, but which does not lather well with soap. To the north-west, north and east of the village, is a range of fair enclosures, consisting of what is called a white malm, a sort of rotten or rubble stone, which, when turned up to the frost and rain, moulders to pieces, and becomes manure to itself.

Still on to the north-east, and a step lower, is a kind of white land, neither chalk nor clay, neither fit for pasture nor for the plough, yet kindly for hops, which root deep into the freestone, and have their poles and wood for charcoal growing just at hand. This white soil produces the brightest hops. As the parish still inclines down towards Wolmer-forest, at the juncture of the clays and sand the soil becomes a wet, sandy loam, remarkable for timber, and infamous for roads. The oaks of Temple and Blackmoor stand high in the estimation of purveyors, and have furnished much naval timber; while the trees on the freestone grow large, but are what workmen call shakey, and so brittle as often to fall to pieces in sawing. Beyond the sandy loam the soil becomes an hungry lean sand, till it mingles with the forest; and will produce little without the assistance of lime and turnips.

QUOTE UNQUOTE

There is a serene and settled majesty to woodland scenery that enters into the soul and delights and elevates it, and fills it with noble inclinations.
Washington Irving, US novelist

LAND-BASED SKIPPERS

Can that be possible? When they're butterflies, it can. There are eight members of the skipper family in Britain – named for the skipping way they flit from plant to plant – the first three of which in this list bear a fairly standard butterfly shape, but the remaining five have an altogether more moth-life appearance, with their forewings folded back and angled up against the hindwings. Beautiful little insects...

Chequered skipper
Dingy skipper
Grizzled skipper
Small skipper
Large skipper
Essex skipper
Silver-spotted skipper
Lulworth skipper

WHAT'S IN A NAME: P

Pallister	Park-keeper
Pantler	Butler
Pargeter	Ornamental plasterer
Picker	Caster of loom shuttles
Pinder	Dog catcher
Poster	Rock breaker in quarries
Puddler	Wrought iron or clay worker

STADDLE STITCHED UP

Staddle stones, those mushroom shaped support structures once used to raise granaries from the ground so that rodents couldn't get in for a quick snack, have become very popular garden ornaments in recent years. So popular, in fact, that more unscrupulous types have realised that they can reach a pretty penny. By the late 1990s, particularly in Wiltshire, thefts of these heavy items (by, presumably, the more musclebound members of the criminal fraternity) were becoming very common.

Until 1999, when one constable from the Wiltshire police force hit upon a good idea. With indelible paint, and the owner's permission, he inked the postcode of the garden in which each stone stood on the underside of its base. It worked, too. On more than one occasion, thieves, having lifted off the top and then presumably noticed the markings on it, simply left the tops in the grass, realising that they wouldn't be able to sell them on.

Bet that made them staddle sore.

A CHAUCER CUT OF CHICKEN

The plot of the Nun's Priest's Tale, from Chaucer's Canterbury Tales, in a nutshell:

A poor old widow lived a simple life with her daughters and their livestock, which included a few chickens and a rooster. Chanticleer by name, he was a proud and lively fellow with many hen-wives, but the one he loved the most was the beautiful Pertelote.

One night Chanticleer has a dream that an orange hound-like beast is threatening to kill him, and the following day he can't shake the sombre mood it puts him in. Pertelote tries to soothe him, but all he can think of are tales of great men who dreamed of murder, only to find it was true. Still, his mood is not too bad: that night he 'feathers' Pertelote 20 times!

Then one day, a fox comes to the pen. The wily rascal praises Chanticleer, and asks to hear him sing. Flattered, the cockerel fluffs himself and raises his head for a chorus, whereupon the fox grabs him around the neck and runs off to the wood. The widow, her daughters and their dogs give chase, but the fox is too quick. So, it turns out, is Chanticleer. He recommends that the fox turn around and boast to his pursuers, and as soon as he does, the cockerel breaks free and flies up into a tree, from which no amount of foxy flattery can bring him down.

The moral is clear: never trust a flatterer.

WORKING DOGS

Lurchers

These are the dogs with a reputation from the darker side of hunting. Originally a cross between the greyhound and hunting dogs, lurchers have long been associated with the poaching community, their ability to follow a scent trail and their bold behaviour making them the 'pot-fillers' so despised by the gamekeepers of the nineteenth century and earlier. Even its name has underworld connotations – it comes from the Latin 'lur', meaning thief.

They really are the all-round hunting dogs, with specialisations depending upon their hybridisation of breeds. Saluki/greyhound or deerhound/greyhound lurchers are often used today for rabbit hunting, while the collie/greyhound lurcher is bred more for its rounding-up abilities, and the whippet/greyhound for its speed. Lurchermen hired to hunt rabbits by landowners often use a ferret to force the rabbit out of the ground, while night-time hunting involved using a bright light to spotlight quarry, and is known as lamping.

This plant brought Stan round to the end of misery (5)

Answer on page 153.

QUOTE UNQUOTE

*Home to us was not a fireside, nor even father and mother and broth-
ers and sisters, but included a village, wide grass fields, spinneys dot-
ted among them, a moat and a brook, all populous with very familiar
denizens, whether two-legged or four-legged or six-legged; and as time
went on and incidents accumulated, spinney, pond, field, tree, and the
rest were written over with a quite unforgettable script.*

Sir William Beach Thomas, war correspondent and country writer

Number of days, in 1919, that the Hungarian working class, many from 133
rural backgrounds, briefly took power in their country

Reminiscences of southern counties country life, as recorded by George Sturt in the late nineteenth century from conversations with his gardener, whom he called Bettesworth:

'Whatever should you think my old gal done last night? I was that hurt – there, I dunno when I bin so hurt as I was when I got down 'ome last night an' see what she'd done!'

I could not imagine what she could have done. She is a short, swarthy, toothless old creature, soft-hearted and patient, and looking as fiercely harmless as a weather-beaten scarecrow. And yet – well, I could not but sympathise with Bettesworth, as he continued –

'Before I come away after dinner yesterday, she ast me if she should hoe the pa'snips. "No", I says, "you leave 'em alone. I'll hoe 'em and cut 'em out, to-night." Well, when I went down after I'd left off here, she says to me, "You can 'ave a rest to-night, Fred. There en't no hoein' for you to do. Come an' 'ave a

look." Well, when I looked, she'd hoed them pa'snips purty near all away; an' not content wi' that, if she 'adn'd gone on at my young cabbage-plants. You knows how nice they was comin' on, sir. She 'adnt left not one in five hunderd of 'em.

It was useless to suggest that the old woman had meant no harm. She had spoilt plants worth, perhaps, three half-crowns, or three days' work, to her husband. 'What can she have been thinking of?' said I.

'There – I dunno. I was that mad! I could ha' knocked her down as free as looked at her! I says to her, '"Anybody 'd think you was a reg'lar born fool." I says. No, sir, I couldn't forget it, all that evenin'; an' I felt I must tell ye of it.'

The Bettesworth Book,
written 1896

THE LAND CLARENCES

Clarence Darrow gained great fame in the US towards the end of the nineteenth century and well into the twentieth as a legal defender of the poor and downtrodden, and his name is still cited today as an icon with ethics towards which lawyers should aspire ('should' being the operative word). His determination to win was legendary, and he often put this down to his tough agricultural upbringing. In fact, he was a firm believer that in comparison with farm life, with its round-the-clock hours and dependency on the climate and sheer elbow grease, legal work was a doddle.

'One very hot day I was distributing and packing down the hay which a stacker was constantly dumping on top of me', he once recalled. 'By noon, I was completely exhausted. That afternoon I left the farm, never to return, and I haven't done a day of hard work since.'

134 *Section number of the Rights of Way Act 1990, concerning ploughing of public rights of way*

A HELPING HAND

Champions of the countryside in their own words:

The **NATIONAL FEDERATION FOR BIOLOGICAL RECORD-ING (NFBR)** is the premier UK organisation for practitioners involved in biological recording.

The NFBR
- Brings together suppliers, managers, and users of information about species, habitats and wildlife sites
- Promotes a forum for discussion and sharing of knowledge and experience
- Promotes the importance of biological information in nature conservation, planning, research and public participation
- Represents the biological recording community

Membership includes individual naturalists, national organisations and recording societies, local records centres and their staff.

www.nfbr.org.uk

WHAT'S IN A NAME: R

Ratoner	Rat catcher
Reeler	Operator of yarn winding machinery
Rickmaster	Captain of the horses
Riddler	Wool stapler
Ripper	Fish seller
Roper	Net or rope maker
Rover	Archer

COUNTRY CONTEMPLATIONS

For ordinary wear, on week-days, he had a white 'smock frock': but on Sundays, or his visits to London, he 'got up' for the occasion, and was something of a dandy in his countrified way. Top boots (yellow tops, and the rest shining black), knee breeches, longish drab waist-coat ('quite drab') and frock-coat; with white kerchief round a high white collar, and black beaver hat – oh, but the farmer took a pride in his best clothes, as he was well entitled to do, when one considers his poverty-stricken childhood. Once, for some now unknown reason, he had a white hat. The fur, clipped off from the old hats, was held to be a good thing to put on a cut finger. It was said that he had to have his hats specially made for him in London because of the great size of his head. But I wonder. Where else was a countryman to get a new beaver hat of any size, in those days?

George Sturt, *William Smith, Potter and Farmer: 1790-1858*

STANDING ROOM ONLY

A dead good idea from Australia may well get adopted in other countries one day. A group of Melbourne farmers in 2005 won the right to open a 'feet-first' graveyard, enabling them to bury bodies vertically. There's none of that coffin business either, the bodies being buried in bio-degradable bags.

The idea is not only to save space, but reduce the grave consequences of human death to the environment. 'When you die, you are returned to the earth with a minimum of fuss and with no paraphernalia that will affect the environment,' the group has stated. There are no maintenance costs, no burning of the 90kg of gas used for cremations, and the cemetery will be able to return to pasture land one day.

POMMES FOR POMS

**Ten good dessert apple varieties to grow
in a British orchard, and their flavour:**

Cox's orange pippin *Sweet*
Discovery *Medium to acidic*
Egremont russet *Sweet*
Fiesta *Sweet*
Greensleeves *Medium*
Idared *Medium*
James Grieve *Medium*
Jonagold *Sweet*
Jupiter *Sweet*
Worcester permain *Sweet*

LAST CHANCE TO SEE

The Soay sheep, a very primitive-looking breed, is probably one of the last links back to the very first sheep that were brought to the British Isles, and with fewer than 700 breeding females left, the breed is classed as vulnerable. Named after the island off the Scottish coast on which it was found (the word Soay itself is Norse for 'sheep island'), the breed is unsurprisingly very hardy, and light of step, making it ideal for conservation grazing.

They have excellent mothering instincts, and are just as happy in woodland as on hillsides. Late lambers, they sometimes don't give birth until well into May, although one old piece of Soay advice has that if you 'put ram to ewe on Bonfire Night, you'll get your lamb on Fool's Day'. No-one knows exactly where the breed first came from, although it does bear a strong resemblance to the mouflon of Corsica, Sardinia and Cyprus.

RUN RABBIT RUN

The novel *Watership Down* by Richard Adams not only introduced the world to the trek by Hazel, Fiver, Bigwig and all from Berkshire to Hampshire, but revealed once and for all that rabbits have a religion. It appears that Frith, the Sun God, created the earth and the stars from his droppings. The creatures lived off the grass that Frith provided, but the great god noticed one day that the family of El-ahrairah, the rabbit prince, were eating all the grass by themselves. Warning the prince that he needed to keep his family under control, Frith was angered when the rabbit replied that his people would do what they wished, as they were the best in the world. Frith therefore gave the other families – the foxes, badgers, stoats and so on – the ability to eat rabbits, sending El-ahrairah off in a panic. But Frith is not a heartless god – he also gives the rabbit the gift of powerful hind legs to help him run from his many enemies.

It's all true, you know.

COUNTRY CONUNDRUMS

A cryptic clue:
Play safe before argument concerning ancient boundary (8)
Answer on page 153.

COUNTRY CONTEMPLATIONS

All that I can boast of in my birth is that I was born in old England. With respect to my ancestors, I shall go no further back than my grandfather, and for this very plain reason, that I never heard talk of any previous to him. He was a day-labourer, and I have heard my father say, that he worked for one farmer from the day of his marriage to that of his death, upwards of forty years. He died before I was born, but I have often slept beneath the same roof that had sheltered him, and where his widow dwelt for seven years after his death. It was a little thatched cottage with a garden before the door. It had but two windows; a damson tree shaded one, and a clump of filberts the other. Here I and my brothers went every Christmas and Whitsuntide, to spend a week or two, and torment the poor old woman with our noise and dilapidations. She used to give us milk and bread for breakfast, and apple pudding for our dinner, and a piece of bread and cheese for supper. Her fire was made of turf cut from the neighbouring heath and her evening light was a rush dipped in grease.

William Cobbett,
Rural Rides

Advice for game birds who may be unsure which hunting seasons apply to them:

If you're a red grouse or ptarmigan	*keep out of sight between*	12 August and 10 December
If you're a wader or snipe	*keep out of sight between*	12 August and 31 January
If you're a black grouse	*keep out of sight between*	20 August and 10 December
If you're wildfowl	*keep out of sight between*	1 September and 31 January
If you're a partridge	*keep out of sight between*	1 September and 1 February
If you're a woodcock	*keep out of sight between*	1 October and 31 January
If you're a pheasant	*keep out of sight between*	1 October and 1 February

WORKING DOGS

Collies

Possibly the most useful working dogs of them all, even their very name, some believe, comes from the Gaelic meaning 'something useful' (although others believe it derives from 'coal', alluding to their black hair). Known by various names – working, English, or farm collie – they were given the name Border collie as recently as 1915, to allude to their successful upbringing in the border regions of the UK. The hardiness of the breed was vital to this success: its tough resilience in craggy areas and wind-swept pastures enabled it to herd sheep in almost all conditions, and it was bred increasingly smaller to perform this function more efficiently. Even the white markings on its fur were bred in to help shepherds find their dogs more easily on dark winter evenings.

Unsurprisingly, farmers were very proud of their tough little friends, often competing with each other to find who owned the best. This inevitably led to sheepdog trials, the first of which was held in Wales in 1873. Today, the breed is also used for cliff and mountain search and rescue operations.

WHY DIDN'T THE MAMMAL
CROSS THE ROAD?

In 2000 the Mammal Society conducted one of the more morbid surveys in zoological monitoring. They wanted to find out which mammals were most frequently killed on the roads of Britain, and teams of volunteers spent the next year counting roadkill (except on trunk roads and motorways – there was little point in adding humans to the list). The identity of the greatest sufferer of road accidents came as little surprise... but who would have thought that more hares die on the roads than rabbits?

Hedgehog	29%
Badger	25%
Fox	19%
Grey squirrel	11%
Brown rat	5%
Hare	3%
Others	8%

THE FARMERS' ARMY

Created in the First World War to help get things done on the land while the men were at war, the Women's Land Army was resurrected for World War II with great success. The average weekly wage for the young women over 18 who rolled up their sleeves and got stuck into the threshing, ploughing, drainage and tractor driving was only £1 12d after deductions, and they worked for a maximum of 50 hours during the summer, 48 in winter. In all, 90,000 women joined the Land Army, and their work, which continued after the war until 1950, kept Britain supplied with food.

Making the transition from city-dweller to agricultural expert was not always easy, though, as this extract from the WLA handbook suggests: 'There are so many obvious things which get forgotten. The volunteer should always be punctual in her hours; she should not smoke about the place, especially in farm buildings; she should shut gates behind her; she should put tools back properly, so that the next person who wants them can find them; she should never leave a job half done just because she finds it difficult.

'A farmer is not made in a month, and, after training, some girls are inclined to try to teach the farmer his business, often with unfortunate results. So if a volunteer has been taught a method different from the farmer's, she should always ask his permission before making the change. Farmers have no time to bother with fussy volunteers. They expect girls who have offered to do the work to carry it out without complaint.'

WHEN A SNAKE IS NOT A SNAKE

Despite its serpentine appearance, the slow worm is actually a legless lizard. But then, isn't that just an alternative description of snakes anyway? Not at all. In addition to a different bone structure, the slow worm has eyelids, like a lizard, and when caught can shed its tail, which wriggles around and distracts its would-be predator. The slow-worm, however, is not able to grow its tail back.

If you don't really want to get close enough to study the creature's eyelid structure for ID purposes, take a glance at its body. The head looks very slightly too large for its body, giving it the appearance of an elongated tadpole. Their colouration can vary from light brown to an almost rusty red, but is more even than an adder's, the female carrying a faint dark line down its back, the male occasionally sporting blueish spots. The zigzaggy stripes of the adder are not present.

QUOTE UNQUOTE

Little ol' boy in the Panhandle told me the other day
you can still make a small fortune in agriculture.
Problem is, you got to start with a large one.
Jim Hightower, Texan radio host

RITE AND WRONG OF SPRING

Walt Disney's *Fantasia* was first shown in 1940, and received very mixed reviews, particularly for its cloyingly chocolate box segment based on Beethoven's *Pastoral Symphony*. A few critics were impressed with the film, but most hated it, not least Igor Stravinsky, the only then living composer of the seven whose music was animated in the film. The reason for his ire was that Disney had completely misinterpreted his music, *The Rite of Spring*, which is about a primal sacrificial rural ritual in which a young girl dances herself to death. Perhaps 'misinterpret' is the wrong word, seeing as Walt could hardly use such depressing and violent pagan imagery in his film. He provided a new interpretation altogether: the evolution of life on earth, from the first appearance of the stars and planet, through the development of single-celled organisms, to amphibious creatures, and finally dinosaurs. The original plan was to keep right on until the evolution of mankind, but this was discarded so as not to upset the ticket-paying millions in the creationist bible belt.

The final segment is today hailed as a brave and ambitious animated effort. Stravinsky, at the time, called it 'an unresisting imbecility'. Still, he picked up $5,000 for the rights.

WHAT'S IN A NAME: S

Sawyer	Timber mill worker
Scrivener	Writer or copyist
Sherman	Cloth nap shearer
Simpler	Herbalist
Skinner	Hide dealer
Slater	Roofer
Sortor	Tailor
Souter	Shoe maker
Sumpter	Porter
Swingler	Flax beater

THE WRIGHT STUFF

Want to be a wheelwright? You'll need the
following tools – as long as they're not spoken for:

Buzz • Boxing engine
Jarvis • Traveller
Adze • Axe • Auger

MEMORIES AND CONVERSATION

Reminiscences of southern counties country life, as recorded by George Sturt in the late nineteenth century from conversations with his gardener, whom he called Bettesworth:

'Up at Forest Pond is where they used to play [cricket] so much. Clifton used to bring up all the booths and things, hot meals and all. 'Cause there wa'n't no pub there then. No, there was no pub there when I was a little boy; but Clifton – they was always a cricketin' fam'ly – he used to bring up the booths... An' didn't there use to be some people there too, on the day o' that match! I've knowed 'm come from all round – Shawbury and Swankley an' Rocknest – more than what there would to a fair! There was a interest in cricket then... An' there was booths all round, an't the crick-

et; and then after that was over, all kinds o' games – kiss-in-the-ring and drop-glove – for the young women, you know. But there wa'n't no pub, only if you wanted anything you could go into the booths and get it.'

The natural conservatism in Bettesworth is appealed to by cricket. It seems to him a good old-fashioned south-country game; and he will generally emphasise his approval of it by observing irrelevantly, 'But this 'ere football, no, I can't see nothing in that. I reckon that's a nasty, dangerous game'.

***The Bettesworth Book,*
written 1896**

GORSE OF COURSE

Northern Ireland's favourite county wild flowers,
according to a Plantlife International survey, are:

Antrim	*Harebell*
Armagh	*Cowbane*
Belfast	*Gorse*
Derry	*Purple saxifrage*
Down	*Spring squill*
Fermanagh	*Globeflower*
Tyrone	*Bog-rosemary*

COUNTRY CONTEMPLATIONS

For any stranger who might have a fancy for seeing the Welsh people in the hours of ease, no better stage could be selected than the shady walks which converge on the pump-room at Llanwrtyd. Five or six times a day, before and after every meal, the long procession of patients and holiday-makers traverses the half mile of road which connects the village and the Dolecoed grounds where they mostly disport themselves. All ages and almost all classes are represented in the motley concourse that, increasing with each July day, keeps up such a regular promenade. Half of them, perhaps, are chattering Welsh and all of them, save a few cripples, are as garrulous and happy as they ought to be when the cares of farm and mine, of pulpit, shop and office are cast aside. Here is a Baptist preacher waving his croquet mallet at his fellow players with much of that authority which the pulpit has made a second nature, oblivious for the time of local politics or the disestablishment of the Church. There is a country parson from North Wales bursting with information on Church statistics and interested in the price of sheep. Here again is a group of young men singing part songs as they stroll along with as much nonchalance and accuracy as if they had imbibed the art with their mothers' milk; there a bench full of Cardiganshire farmers talking chapels and crops, any one of whom would be painfully disconcerted if called upon at a moment's notice for a complete sentence of English. The Mothers of Wales are here too of course with their knitting, those capacious, determined looking matrons I have so often alluded to with unstinted admiration. What a fine holiday it must be for them too, chickens and milkcows, calves and pigs, wash tubs and sewing machines, all abandoned for a whole blessed fortnight, or even for a month. No woman in the world must surely enjoy a change quite so thoroughly as a working farmer's wife.

A G Bradley,
*Highways and Byways
in South Wales,* 1914

PECKING ORDER

Everyone's heard of the Rhode Island red, but there are many other chicken breeds. Here are some examples, but beware, the list is not eggs-austive:

Appenzell bearded hen
Buttercup
Delaware
Gimmizah
Minorca
Naked neck
Plymouth Rock
Silver montazah
Wyandottes

COUNTRY CONUNDRUMS

A cryptic clue:
Endlessly Hagrid is followed by society's ways of farming (11)
Answer on page 153.

A HELPING HAND

Champions of the countryside in their own words:

The **CAMPAIGN FOR THE PROTECTION OF RURAL ENGLAND (CPRE)** are people who care passionately about our countryside and campaign for it to be protected and enhanced for the benefit of everyone. The countryside is one of England's most important resources but its beauty, tranquillity and diversity are threatened in many different ways.

We are a registered charity with about 59,000 members and supporters. They live in cities and towns as well as villages and the countryside. Anyone who supports our aims is encouraged to join.

We operate as a network with over 200 district groups, a branch in every county, a group in every region and a national office, making CPRE a powerful combination of effective local action and strong national campaigning.

We are one of the longest established and most respected environmental groups, influencing policy and raising awareness ever since we were founded in 1926.

www.cpre.org.uk

Lady Muriel, newly crowned cheerleading champion of West Oxon, was prone to practising her baton-twirling at the most inappropriate of times.

WORKING DOGS

Otterhounds

Since the otter was first placed on the Endangered Species list in 1978, the dog that was bred to hunt it has almost vanished from the British Isles. The otterhound can be traced back to the twelfth century, probably being bred from the bloodhound and other hound strains, as well as the French griffon. A pack hound, it is a fine swimmer with an excellent nose, and was a favourite of royals, otter-hunting reaching a peak of popularity in the late nineteenth century.

The hound is still put to the hunt, however... not for otters any more, but mink, an invasive species that has developed several feral colonies in Britain from escapes from furfarms in the mid-twentieth century.

Otterhounds are the dogs seen in the film *Tarka the Otter*.

THE WORST FARMER EVER?

A good candidate for the award must be the young man who, back in the mid-seventeenth century, was taken out of school by his mother to run the family farm. He was hopeless. Once, when he was supposed to be watching the livestock, he was found curled up under a hedge with a good book. Another time when he was supposed to be taking the produce to market, he was seen trying jumping experiments, to determine how forceful the wind was.

By the time his mother gave up on him, she'd lost some of the cattle, and no-one knew where the eggs were. But at least he had a full notebook of scribblings, including recipes for clearing the brain, a formula for making chalk, observations about the stars above, and a method for making gold ink.

The young man's name was Isaac Newton.

COUNTRY CONTEMPLATIONS

What a scene was that corn-field under the hot August sky! Fiery red glowed the faces of the harvestmen, against the golden back-ground, a sea of waving wheat, the famed ruddy-hued wheat of Talavera. Not a cloud obscured the burning blue heavens, whilst beyond the standing corn showed here and there a bit of foliage, lofty hedge starred with wild roses or low pollard oaks of deep rich green.

As the afternoon drew on the sultriness increased, and these brilliant contrasts of colour grew more intense. Southern warmth and gorgeousness seemed to invest that Suffolk harvest field. But the bucolic mood of the reapers had passed. As the sickles moved automatically backwards and forwards, not a word passed their lips, a regiment of deaf mute were hardly quieter. From time to time, at a signal of the leader, each stood up, wiped his brow, shook himself, took a draught of beer, interchanged a word with his fellow, then resumed work vigorously as before.

The sun sank behind the pollard oaks and twilight succeeded, hardly bringing coolness. A little later, although no breeze sprang up, pleasant freshness lightened their labours; another and yet another drink from the master's can lent new strength, long after moon rising, that mechanical swing of twenty arms, that gleam of twenty sickles went on. Deep, almost solemn silence reigned over the corn-field. Only the rustle of footsteps and wheat falling on the stover broke the stillness, a stillness and monotony emblematic of these noiseless, unheroic lives, the tide of human existence that perpetually ebbs and flows, leaving no memory behind.

Matilda Betham Edwards,
The Lord of the Harvest, 1899

QUOTE UNQUOTE

To the lost man, to the pioneer penetrating a new country, to the naturalist who wishes to see the wild land at its wildest, the advice is always the same – follow a river. The river is the original forest highway. It is nature's own Wilderness Road.
Edwin Way Teale, US naturalist

REED ON

Want to be a thatcher? Get yourself the following tools, and you'll be covered:

Knee pad
Leggat
Opening tool
Needle
Pin
Reed hook
Clasp-knife
Eaves knife
Mallet

COUNTRY CONTEMPLATIONS

I think it will not be an over-statement to say my father was one of the first to retail milk in Wootton Bassett.

Just to think of it! 1/2 pennyworths and pennyworths of milk, fresh, uncooled from the cow. Very well, having disposed of what people asked for en route to home there was the daily need of the home and business to be catered for. This quite naturally varied and there were surpluses sometimes. In such cases it was put into setting pans, skimmed and the cream made into butter. [My sister] Gertie spent hours with a very primitive sort of butter maker. It was not a churn, but a large tin with a plunger which fitted loosely inside, and had holes through which the cream was forced by means of the handle which enabled it to be pulled up, and forced down.

Mother would then come into the picture, and made the butter up into pats and either used in the home or sold to customers. Again, another problem, what's to be done with the skimmed milk? Nothing could be better for pigs, so as pigs of 8 weeks old could at that time be bought for a few shillings each, Dad used to buy about eight and feed them on to bacon weights of about 9 to 10 score. When fit for the local butcher, they were killed in the yard and the hair burned off in beds of straw.

The Written Memories of Ernest Charlie Tayler, recording the Edwardian years in Wiltshire

A HELPING HAND

Champions of the countryside in their own words:

THE TREE COUNCIL was founded in 1974 with major support from the Department of the Environment, and in 1978 became an independent registered charity.

The Tree Council's aims are:
- To improve the environment in town and country by promoting the planting and conservation of trees and woods throughout the United Kingdom.
- To disseminate knowledge about trees and their management.
- To act as a forum for organisations concerned with trees, to identify national problems and to provide initiatives for co-operation.

www.treecouncil.org.uk

COUNTRY CONUNDRUMS

A cryptic clue:
Place sand around view (9)
Answer on page 153.

MEMORIES AND CONVERSATION

Reminiscences of southern counties country life, as recorded by George Sturt in the late nineteenth century from conversations with his gardener, whom he called Bettesworth:

A wedding in the village was being celebrated by a most wanton ding-donging of the church bells. I remarked on the wastefulness of spending money on mere noise, and on so much of it; but Bettesworth explained that the bridegroom was one of the village bell-ringers. And, he said, 'The ringers always does like that, if there's e'er a one of 'em 'appens to git married. They was all down about he's 'ome, I see, when I come up by.'

'Still, some people will spend without that excuse at a wedding.'

'Jest to make a day of it. So they will: anything to make a day. An' then they wants before the week's out... Now these 'ere bank 'olidays, I don't think they ever was meant for the likes o' we. Years ago there wa'n't nothing o' that kind. They was meant for clerks in big firms – what spends their time in office an' never gits out o' doors, not for we. We be always workin' out o' doors an' keeps our health an' we don't want 'em. There never used to be none of it, an' now when it comes to three or four days follerin'... But 't is all very well for clerks'.

The Bettesworth Book, 1896

Day by day, Oliver was being driven steadily madder by the voices of the phantom pheasants: '...and after they ban hunting, they'll close the post office, then they'll build a big supermarket right where you're standing, and then...'

WHAT'S IN A NAME: W

Wainwright	Maker or repairer of wagons
Wanter	Mole catcher
Warrener	Rabbit catcher
Washman	Tin plater
Wheeler	Either a wheel-maker, or someone who led pit ponies underground
Whig	Horse driver
Whitesmith	Tinsmith

REIGN DEER

Britain's six species of deer have been here for varying lengths of time:

Red deer   *Indigenous*
Roe deer   *Indigenous*
Fallow deer   *Eleventh century, introduced by the Normans*
Sika   *1860, introduced to deer parks*
Chinese water deer *1873, brought to London Zoo*
Reeves Muntjac   *1894, introduced to Woburn Park*

In addition, the reindeer, extinct for about 8000 years, was introduced into the Cairngorms in 1952, where some still live in a controlled breeding programme today.

SHAM POOH

The *Hundred Acre Wood*: a woodland hidey-hole where the creatures of the forest – plus an amiable old bear called Pooh – go about their days in a mixture of friendship and innocent fun. Right? Wrong, according to a group of Canadian neurodevelopmentalists, who have found something altogether more disturbing in this product of AA Milne's mind. Pooh, for example, bears every indication of suffering from Attention Deficit Hyperactivity Disorder, as well as comorbid cognitive impairment. In fact his relentless pursuit of honey suggests an Obsessive Compulsive Disorder to boot. The authors of the article, which was published in the Canadian Medical Journal in 2000, wonder whether some of these issues may have come about as a result of being dragged repeatedly down the stairs.

Piglet, of course, shows every sign of General Anxiety Disorder, while the chronic dysthymia of Eeyore makes him in urgent need of antidepressants. Rabbit is over-bearing and self-important, leading the authors to conclude that he might best be suited to a role in hospital administration; Kanga is over-protective and suffers from an environment with no comparable female role models; while Roo, while young and excitable now, is on course for disappointment in later life, his single-parent family putting him in risk of a Poorer Outcome future. Christopher Robin, of course, spends far too much of his time talking to animals.

And what of Tigger? He demonstrates a recurring pattern of risk-taking behaviour (a bad role model for Roo), is socially intrusive, excessively hyperactive and impulsive, and is in urgent need of medication.

And you thought that neurodevelopmentalists had no sense of humour!

Some avian collective nouns:

Capercaillies	*Tok*
Finches	*Charm*
Goshawk	*Flight*
Redwings	*Crowd*
Shelducks	*Dopping*
Woodpeckers	*Escent*

COUNTRY CONTEMPLATIONS

Early in that decade of long hot summers which reached its peak with the Paul Nash skies of the Battle of Britain a young couple took their family from market town to farm. The eighteenth century farmhouse, with its cat-slide roof and front porch at the back, hid behind its protective row of elm trees and faced south towards the northern escarp-ment of the Marlborough Downs. The new freedom allowed the children to burst like seeds from a pod into the wel-coming fields. Trees became homes, the brown brook was a Congo, or Tennessee Valley dam, and clay from a digging made home-baked marbles. Rook shoots were neighbourhood gatherings. Hedge-trimmings made a monster Guy Fawkes bonfire. Old hayricks became trampolines for somersaulting. Ancient rubbish mounds, treas-ure trove. Mushrooms were gathered. Cowslips tired them with the picking. Blackberries fought the purple fingers. Little red apples tantalised. A tree house was built.

For the parents it was a different story. Unknown to them, disease was endemic and calves died from contagious abortion. A son was born, lived two happy years, and died. His mother took to her horse and rode out grief over the hills. The couple worked on, but with a powerful goal, that of giving their children opportunities in life that had not been available to them-selves. With generations of farming ancestors behind them they laboured with increasing success.

Comfrey and meadowsweet marked the roadside ditches. Kingcups and brandy-bottles glowed along the wandering line of the brook. Yellow flag iris and bulrushes marked the marshy places where in the spring one could hardly walk for fear of treading on the frogs which showered upward. Wild nature had not been affected by those man-suffered losses and griefs.

Olive Tait,
Barnhill Farm

DURING THE COMPILATION OF THIS BOOK, THE COMPANION TEAM...

Raised 17 chickens, and lost 12 of them to the vicissitudes of nature, four to old age, and one to some sort of supernatural power

Visited 12 farms for research, and while there, tucked into no fewer than 29 full English breakfasts

Got lost in three woodlands, surviving only thanks to the breadcrumbs that leaked through the holes in their pockets

Decided that the difference between a townie and a countrysider was nothing more than attitude, perception and an accident of birth

Realised that if Harvey met Esther you'd have a combine harvester

Saw 33 species of butterfly during one season

Became increasingly impressed with the fortitude of the old rural folk

Climbed nine trees, falling out of eight of them, breaking no limbs, and deciding miracles can happen

Explored the poetry of John Clare and wondered if it could be written today

Counted 4,322 ladybird spots

Got rained on 19 times, hailed on five times, but still got up the next morning

Stared for 34 hours across various parts of the British countryside and knew that there was no better place to be

Please note that although every effort has been made to ensure accuracy in this book, the above statistics may be the result of wandering minds.

The countryside is the most precious natural resource England possesses.

Max Hastings

The answers. As if you needed them.

P13. *Countryfile*

P22. One big one

P24. Helm (silver birch and elm)

P33. Countryside

P38. James Herriot

P43. Brook

P49. Selfheal

P54. Minister for the Environment

P61. Aberdeen Angus

P64. Dandelion

P69. Meacher

P79. A garganey is a duck. The others are all names of lengths of Cotswold slate.

P86. Mallow

P87. Hen

P91. c) £5

P103. Silo

P107. Countryside Act

P112. Scots Pine

P120. It was the first line spoken (by Peggy Skilbeck) in the first episode of Emmerdale Farm (16 October 1972).

P124. Rustic

P133. Tansy

P137. Hedgerow

P143. Agriculture

P147. Landscape

To err is human, to moo, bovine.

Anon

ACKNOWLEDGEMENTS

We gratefully acknowledge permission to reprint extracts of copyright material in this book from the following authors, publishers and executors:

Nature Cure by Richard Mabey, published by Chatto & Windus. Reprinted by permission of The Random House Group Ltd.
Nature Cure by Richard Mabey, published by Chatto and Windus. Copyright © Richard Mabey 2005. Reproduced by permission of Sheil Land Associates Ltd.

In Search of Nature by DA Ratcliffe reproduced by permission of the author.

The Countryside: Random Gleanings by Ralph Whitlock, published by The Gavin Press. Reproduced by permission of Pollinger Limited and the proprietor.

Number of sheep slaughtered due to foot and mouth at Feckenham, 157
Worcestershire, on 2 March 2001

INDEX

The Birdwatcher's Companion Twitchers, birders and ornithologists are all catered for in this unique book. ISBN 1-86105-833-0

The Cook's Companion Foie gras or fry-ups, this tasty compilation is an essential ingredient in any kitchen. ISBN 1-86105-772-5

The Countryside Companion From milking stools to crofters tools, this book opens the lid on the rural scene. ISBN 1-86105-918-3

The Fishing Companion This fascinating catch of fishy facts offers a whole new angle on angling. ISBN 1-86105-919-1

The Gardener's Companion For anyone who has ever gone in search of flowers, beauty and inspiration. ISBN 1-86105-771-7

The Golfer's Companion From plus fours to six irons, here's where to find the heaven and hell of golf. ISBN 1-86105-834-9

The History of Britain Companion All the oddities, quirks, origins and stories that make our country what it is today. ISBN 1-86105-914-0

The Ideas Companion The stories behind the trademarks, inventions, and brands that we come across every day. ISBN 1-86105-835-7

The Legal Companion From lawmakers to lawbreakers, find out all the quirks and stories behind the legal world. ISBN 1-86105-838-1

The Literary Companion Literary fact and fiction from Rebecca East to Vita Sackville-West. ISBN 1-86105-798-9

The London Companion Explore the history and mystery of the most exciting capital city in the world. ISBN 1-86105-799-7

The Moviegoer's Companion Movies, actors, cinemas and salty popcorn in all their glamorous glory. ISBN 1-86105-797-0

The Politics Companion Great leaders and greater liars of international politics gather round the hustings. ISBN 1-86105-796-2

The Sailing Companion Starboards, stinkpots, raggie and sterns – here's where to find out more. ISBN 1-86105-839-X

The Shakespeare Companion A long, hard look at the man behind the moustache and his plethora of works. ISBN 1-86105-913-2

The Traveller's Companion For anyone who's ever stared at a plane and spent the day dreaming of faraway lands. ISBN 1-86105-773-3

The Walker's Companion Ever laced a sturdy boot and stepped out in search of stimulation? This book is for you. ISBN 1-86105-825-X

The Wildlife Companion Animal amazements and botanical beauties abound in this book of natural need-to-knows. ISBN 1-86105-770-9